INSIGHT

D0779829

CAYMAN ISLANDS

Discovery
CHANNEL

APA PUBLICATIONS

Part of the Langenscheidt Publishing Group

L

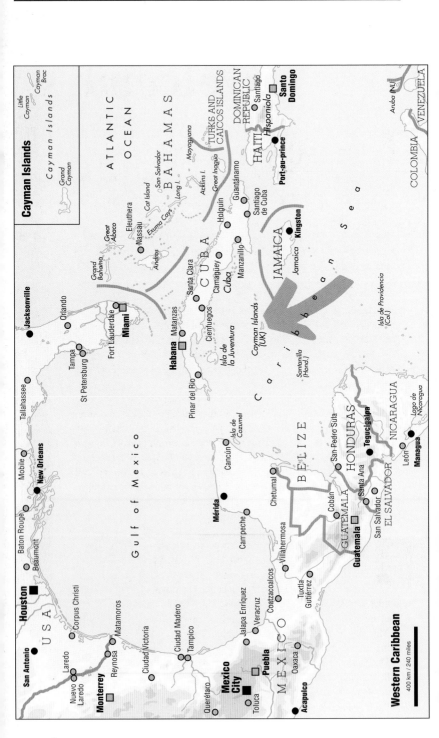

Western Caribbean

introduction

Welcome

This guidebook combines the interests and enthusiasm of two of the world's best-known information providers: Insight Guides, who have set the standard for visual travel guides since 1970, and Discovery Channel, the world's premier source of documentary television programming. Its aim is to show readers the best of the Cayman Islands during the course of a series of itineraries devised by Joann Biondi, one of Insight's main correspondents in the Caribbean.

For over 40 years, the Cayman Islands has attracted travelers drawn to the destination's spectacular scuba-diving sites, sophisticated way of life, and casual ambiance. Just 480 miles (772 km) south of Miami, this trio of tropical islands sitting in the crystal-clear Caribbean Sea is a sweet melange of West Indian sassiness, British sensibility, and multicultural cohesiveness. Grand Cayman, the largest of the three, is known throughout the world for its responsible scuba-diving industry, powdery sand beaches, first-class resorts, fine dining, nightlife, and duty-free shopping. The smaller sisters, Cayman Brac and Little Cayman, are environmentally friendly scuba havens with pristine beaches as well, but they are also great escapes from the rigors of the modern world.

The first nine itineraries in this guide concentrate on Grand Cayman, with tours to the bustling capital, historic attractions, the world's only commercial turtle farm, quaint towns, submarine trips, and favorite scuba sites. They are followed by excursions to Cayman Brac and Little Cayman, with four itineraries highlighting things to see and do on those islands, along with round-ups of their most popular scuba sites. The itineraries are supported by sections on history and culture, shopping, eating out, nightlife, a calendar of events, and a detailed practical information that includes a list of hand-picked hotels.

 Joann Biondi, a former newspaper reporter, has spent many years writing about the Caribbean for numerous magazines. A veteran Apa correspondent, she has written seven books for Insight Guides, and teaches Cultural Geography and Travel and Tourism at Miami-Dade Community College. She lives in Miami, which she says is the next best thing to living in the Caribbean.

This edition is kept up-to-date by Lindsey Turnbull, originally from the UK, she is a long time resident of the Cayman Islands. Lindsey is the editor of the *Cayman Islands Journal*.

HISTORY AND CULTURE

From the early days of settlement and piracy, through the years as a dependency of Jamaica, to the 20th-century decision to become a British Crown Colony – a look at the factors that have shaped the islands **11**

ITINERARIES

The first nine tours explore the essential sights and main activities for visitors to Grand Cayman. The following four take in the highlights of neighboring Cayman Brac (tours 10 and 11) and Little Cayman (tours 12 and 13).

Pages 2/3: an underwater encounter with a grouper
Pages 8/9: dropping anchor at Seven Mile Beach

MORGAN LE FLIBUSTIER

&*History* *Culture*

Like most of the Caribbean, the Cayman Islands have a history inextricably linked to Christopher Columbus, who, on his fourth and final voyage to the New World in 1503, recorded spotting the two small islands now known as Cayman Brac and Little Cayman. Because they were teeming with huge, green sea turtles, he called them *Las Tortugas.*

Unlike most other Caribbean islands, however, there were no indigenous Amerindians living here at the time so no conquest ever took place. In fact, Columbus and his men were so busy repairing their leaky ships and trying desperately to make landfall in Jamaica that they never even set foot in the Cayman Islands. Why there were no indigenous people here remains a mystery. Nearby Jamaica, Cuba, and Haiti all had large Amerindian populations. Historians can only guess that members of the various indigenous groups – Carib, Ciboney, Taíno, and Arawak – who must have paddled by in their dugout canoes, considered the flat, arid islands, which had no rivers or lakes, to be too difficult a place to try to forge a life.

During the next 100 years the turtles on the islands became a much-needed food supply for mariners on their way from Jamaica to America. Along with making a sweet-tasting meal, the turtle meat also helped prevent the onslaught of scurvy, and, since they could be kept alive on board ships for months at a time, they also proved to be a convenient staple for the long journeys home to Europe. The name *Las Tortugas*, given by Columbus, did not stick, however, and instead the islands became known as Caymanas. The new name, a Carib Amerindian word meaning crocodile, was just as appropriate, since, along with the turtles, there were thousands of crocodiles inhabiting the islands. After being hunted and eaten by passing sailors for over 300 years, the crocodile population eventually dwindled down to almost zero, but they left the legacy of their name.

Settlers, Slaves, and Pirates

Although they were used as a place to rest and gather food, the Cayman Islands did not receive permanent settlers until the latter half of the 17th century. Oliver Cromwell gained control of Jamaica from the Spanish in 1655, and English dominance of the Cayman Islands soon followed. Then, in 1670, the Treaty of Madrid formally granted English ownership. During the next 100 years the population grew to about 500, including British soldiers, planters, loggers, rope-makers, ship-builders, and a modest number of African slaves. The early settlers, English, Scots and Welsh, did not have an easy life. The harsh, isolated, and inhospitable environment, that was

Left: Sir Henry Morgan, a notorious scoundrel, enjoying life afloat
Right: a 16th-century painting of Columbus

often hit by tropical storms and brutal hurricanes, meant that the harvesting of corn, cotton, yams, plantains, oranges, and limes was a grueling task. It also meant that the settlers were totally dependent on passing ships for other provisions as well as for news from the rest of the world.

Then there was the constant threat of attack from unsavory characters – shipwrecked mariners, army deserters, Spanish conquistadors, and just plain nasty old pirates who considered the entire region a free-for-all, where they marauded with flagrant greed and grabbed whatever they pleased. Among

the more notorious scoundrels who roamed the waters offshore were Sir Henry Morgan, Sir Edward Teach (better known as Blackbeard), and Ann Bonney, one of the few women pirates who ever made it into the history books. Bonney was a member of 'Calico Jack' Rackham's gang when she was arrested and imprisoned in Jamaica. It was from this checkered past of villainous pirates that grand and convoluted tales of buried treasure and hidden skeletons took root throughout the islands.

By 1802 the population had risen to almost 1,000, about half of whom were enslaved Africans. Compared to other nearby islands, where the enslaved population at times constituted over 80 percent, the Cayman Islands never developed into a full-fledged plantation economy fueled by slave labor. Modern historians claim that this is probably the reason why there has never been any serious racial tension or unrest in the Islands.

In 1832, the residents of Grand Cayman gathered at St James Castle and voted to create a legislature of representatives. In 1834 the British Parliament passed an act declaring the emancipation of all enslaved people and the following year all those held in bondage in Cayman were freed. Many of the former slaves either moved to unclaimed land in the interior of the islands, or settled on small parcels of land given to them by their former masters. Others moved to the nearby Bay Islands of Honduras, in the south.

Throughout the 1800s, settlers focused on building a local infrastructure that included schools and churches. It wasn't until the 1830s that small, permanent communities began to spring up on Little Cayman and Cayman Brac. For the most part, local men earned a living as sailors and ship-builders, as fishermen or turtle-harvesters. A few went off to work on the construction of the Panama Canal. Most Caymanian women took care of the homes, raised the children and made thatch-palm products – hats, brooms, and

Above: Sir Edward Teach, the English privateer who was more commonly known as Blackbeard the Pirate baskets – that they sold locally at markets and exported abroad. The Imperial Act of 1863 formally made the Cayman Islands a dependency of Jamaica, and for the next 20 years the economy flourished, with farming, cattle-rearing, coconut-growing, phosphate-mining, and rope-making.

At the turn of the 20th century the population hit the 5,000 mark, but about 1,500 of these were Caymanian men who frequently left the islands for years at a time to work as merchant marines. In the early 1900s a network of roads was built in Grand Cayman, connecting the various communities on the island. It was also during the early years of the 20th century that the first public buildings were constructed.

In 1953 and 1954 the first airstrips were built on Grand Cayman and Cayman Brac, laying the groundwork for what would become the golden egg of tourism. A few years later tourist hotels were built on Seven Mile Beach and in 1957 dive operator Bob Soto established the first recreational dive shop on Grand Cayman. It was this operation that first introduced visitors to the amazing wonders beneath the calm, aquamarine waters offshore.

Tax-free Status

The Cayman Islands continued to be a dependency of Jamaica until 1962, when the latter chose to become an independent nation and the people of the Cayman Islands voted to hold tight to the Union Jack and become a British Crown Colony instead. Unlike Jamaica, which had a larger population, a vast amount of natural resources, and a rich and fertile landscape capable of producing coffee and sugar, the Cayman Islands saw the prospect of independence as too daunting. Instead, the islands looked toward offshore banking and tourism as their means of economic survival.

In 1966, landmark legislation was passed that paved the way for the development of the banking industry and tax-free status of the islands. Some local historians, however, claim that this concept of tax-free status dates back to 1788, when a convoy of 10 ships carrying merchants from Jamaica to England was wrecked off Grand Cayman and local people rushed to their rescue. King George III of England showed his appreciation for the daring rescue by decreeing the islands a tax-free haven.

In 1967 the national carrier, Cayman Airways, first took to the air; and in 1972 a new constitution was introduced, granting the Cayman Islands autonomy on most domestic issues.

From 1970 to 2005 the islands' population grew from about 10,000 to just over 44,000. The growth in both the banking and tourism industries has been so phenomenal that there is no longer a need for financial assistance from Great Britain. The Cayman Islands has become a well-respected hub of international finance during the past three decades or so. With more than 500 international banks in operation, mostly in Grand Cayman, it is now the fifth largest financial center in the world. It is also the world's biggest offshore-island financial center and one of the largest insurance hubs, with about 400 insurance companies maintaining a base in Grand Cayman.

Grand Cayman is home to some top lawyers, accountants and bankers. Using this skilled base and directed by legislation, along with its neutral tax regime, financial services in the Cayman Islands such as captive insurance, hedge and mutual funds have flourished. Although the country has a good reputation within the international financial services community, feature films such as *The Firm*, based on John Grisham's novel, damaged public perception of the place. The 1993 movie had a plot that included a law firm whose mob clients laundered their cash in the islands.

With the success of the financial services industry came development and during the 1970s and 1980s thousands of modern concrete homes, apartments, condos and hotels were built throughout Grand Cayman, as well as smaller homes and hotels on Cayman Brac.

In 1978 the islands passed the Marine Conservation law, recognizing the importance of the marine environment as a natural resource. Eight years later, in 1986, the Marine Parks Laws were passed, with the aim of replenishing the marine environment by protecting the coral reefs and marine breeding grounds and regulating activities in and around the islands' waters. In 1987 the National Trust for the Cayman Islands was established as an independent

body to work with the government and local communities in an effort to preserve the local culture, history, flora, fauna, wildlife, and marine environment.

Since then the trust has worked diligently at preserving historic buildings and sites, opening museums, establishing public parks and nature preserves, and protecting public access to beaches and the sea. In 1994 James Manoah Bodden was officially named the first National Hero of the islands. Bodden, a prominent government leader, was primarily responsible for the founding of Cayman Airways and the modernization of Grand Cayman's Owen Roberts International Airport.

Jobs for All

Today, the Cayman Islands enjoys the highest standard of living and the highest per capita income in all the Caribbean (about US$36,000), and there is practically no unemployment. Strict immigration laws mean that all jobs in the islands must first be offered to a Caymanian and only if there are no local residents available or willing to fill the positions can the work be offered to foreigners, who must obtain a work permit from the government. There are so many well-paid jobs that many of the less lucrative service positions are filled by immigrants. There are sizeable numbers of Jamaicans, Canadians, Australians, Britons and Americans working in the tourism industry. The cost of living, however, is high and consumer goods – cars, houses, clothing, electronics, and foods – are relatively expensive. Also high-priced are the costs of utility services such as telephones, electricity, and Internet service provision.

With over 1.2 million visitors a year, the Cayman Islands is well established as a major, mass-market tourist destination. The first impression that a visitor is likely to have of the place is that of an affluent hamlet. A safe, peaceful,

Above: turtles still flourish at the Cayman Turtle Farm

well-managed trio of islands with a sense of British efficiency and old-fashioned manners. Similar in many ways to Bermuda, the Cayman Islands' infrastructure is first-rate and up-to-date and works extremely well. For a group of tiny, isolated islands they are indeed a modern-day success story. There are no visible inner-city slums, no poverty in the countryside, no homeless people, no beggars, and no street hustlers harassing tourists, as can be seen elsewhere in the region. Nor are there any gambling casinos, a characteristic linked to the fact that the conservative-minded Christian churches on the islands hold a great deal of sway.

Birds and Beasts

Away from the concrete ribbon of modern hotels and high-rise condos that line Grand Cayman's Seven Mile Beach, there are still many pristine places to be found, where local people are eager to talk to visitors and the pace of life is molasses slow. Old, tropical-style cottages with breezy verandahs and bold Caribbean colors dot many nooks and crannies away from the main tourist areas. And even a few traditional wattle and daub houses remain. Although no longer built, these old homes were constructed with iron-wood posts, woven cabbage-wood walls, and a thick mortar called daub that was used to coat the entire structure. Extremely labor-intensive to construct, the houses were sturdy enough to withstand hurricanes.

Turtles have always lived on the islands. As we know, Columbus mentioned them in his log and named the islands after them, and turtle farming remains an important industry. Still abundant, due to a successful breeding program at the Cayman Turtle Farm, the large, green sea turtle is a national symbol and its image can be found on flags, currency, souvenirs, the official government seal and even on the jets in the Cayman Airways fleet.

What is most striking about the Cayman Islands, and the reason why most people come here, is how Mother Nature struts her stuff. First of all there's the sea and the kaleidoscope of colors that lie beneath it – stunning coral reefs, dramatic walls,

Above: the Little Cayman iguana is probably the most striking of the indigenous creatures. **Right:** a vividly-colored parrot, one of numerous exotic birds winding ravines, pinnacles, caves, sponges, sea fans, hermit crabs, starfish, sharks, and an array of tropical fish that cause the jaws of even the best-traveled divers to drop in awe. Next comes the bright yellow sun that shines virtually non-stop throughout the year. And then there is the tropical landscape and the unusual creatures that inhabit it.

The islands are blessed with a natural bounty of flora and fauna. There are mangrove swamps, red birch, tropical ferns, bamboo and pine. The indigenous tall slender silver thatch palm is a national symbol, which can be found at the eastern ends of all three islands and until the 1960s it was used for roofing and weaving. Here too are coconut groves, bananas, figs, royal poinciana trees, wild sorrel, hibiscus, frangipani, heliconia, bird of paradise, anthuriums, morning glory vines, cactus, orchids, and bromeliads. The wild banana orchid is another island symbol, one variety, which flowers on Grand Cayman has small scented, white with purple-tipped flowers, with a yellowish version on the sister islands. Among the creatures to look out for are the Grand Cayman and Cayman Brac parrots, endemic birds with iridescent green feathers and reddish-orange necks that live in the interior of the islands and feed on berries from the interestingly named gumbo limbo tree.

About 20,000 red-footed boobies live primarily on Little Cayman and snowy egrets, frigates, humming birds, doves, herons, ospreys, swallows, terns, warblers, woodpeckers, black-headed stilts, quits, vireos, plovers, ducks, owls, and thrushes can all be found just about everywhere. There are also more than 50 species of butterfly and during the summer months their white, fluttering bodies fill the air.

Magnificent Iguanas

A small, rabbit-like animal called an agouti can often be spotted scurrying around densely wooded areas; and frogs, bats, centipedes, caterpillars, nocturnal geckos, mongooses, and non-poisonous snakes are also common. But the most exotic and strikingly handsome creature is, without a doubt, the

iguana. Grand Cayman is home to the endangered and endemic Blue Iguana and locals claim that there are only about 150 of them living in the wild along the eastern end of the island. On Little Cayman there are about 2,000 Little Cayman Rock Iguanas that can grow up to 6ft (2 m) long. On this tiny island, they are often seen strolling around as if they own the joint. Usually slow-moving and lazy, they can be found foraging through the mangroves in search of ripe papayas that have fallen from the surrounding trees.

When visitors come upon them, the iguanas just ignore the interruption and go about their business.

Above: welcome to the Cayman Islands

HISTORY HIGHLIGHTS

1503 Christopher Columbus sights the islands and names them *Las Tortugas* (meaning turtles, in Spanish). Over the next 100 years, the name Cayman comes into common usage.

1586 A fleet of 23 ships, under the direction of privateer, Sir Frances Drake, stops for two days in Grand Cayman. The islands are uninhabited, but Drake makes note of the many turtles, crocodiles, alligators, and iguanas he sees.

1670 Under the terms of the Treaty of Madrid, Spain recognizes England's sovereignty over Jamaica and the Cayman Islands.

1773 The population reaches 400, and the Royal Navy makes its first map of Grand Cayman.

1790 Fort George is constructed to ward off attacks by the French and Spanish.

1794 The 'Wreck of the Ten Sails' take place off the coast of Grand Cayman.

1831 A decision is made to form a new assembly, and the islands' first legislation is passed. The population reaches 2,000.

1830s First missionaries from the Anglican Church arrive. A church is built in George Town, and the first schools are established.

1835 Governor Sligo of Jamaica lands in Cayman to declare all enslaved people free, in accordance with the Emancipation Act of 1833.

1863 An Act of the Imperial Parliament in London declares the Cayman Islands a dependency of Jamaica.

1898 Frederick Sanguinetti, an official of the Jamaican Government, is appointed the first Commissioner of the Cayman Islands.

1911 The population reaches 5,500.

1920 Education Act passes, providing for schools in all districts.

1937 The first cruise ship, the *Atlantis*, sails into port and tourism takes hold.

1940–45 A US Naval and a Coast Guard base are set up on Grand Cayman.

1953 The airport opens in Grand Cayman, replacing the old seaplane base.

1950s Dozens of new hotels open throughout the island

1957 Bob Soto establishes the first recreational diving operation in the Caribbean on Grand Cayman.

1959 Caymanian women are granted the right to vote; the Cayman Islands cease to be a dependency of Jamaica.

1962 Following Jamaica's independence from Great Britain, the Cayman Islands choose to remain a Crown Colony.

1966 Landmark banking legislation is introduced, paving the way for the tax-free status of the islands.

1967 Cayman Airways, the national carrier, takes to the air.

1972 The new Caymanian Constitution is introduced.

1978 Cayman Islands passes the Marine Conservation Law to protect offshore waters.

1986 The Marine Parks Law goes into effect, further insuring protection of marine life in the islands.

1987 The National Trust is created to preserve the natural, historic, and maritime heritage of the islands.

1994 James Manoah Bodden, government leader and co-founder of Cayman Airways, is designated the country's first National Hero.

2000 Jean-Michel Cousteau is named official spokesperson for diving in the Cayman Islands.

2003 The Cayman Islands celebrates its quincentennial year.

2004 One of the strongest storms in a decade, Hurricane Ivan, batters Grand Cayman. The population of the Cayman Islands reaches more than 40,000.

Grand Cayman

3 km / 2 miles

CARIBBEAN SEA

Grape Tree Point

North Side

Old Man Bay

Old Robin Point

Anchor Point

Brinkleys

Old Savannah

Hutland

Old Crawl

Long Point

A 3

Little Bluff

Rogers Wreck Point

Old Man Bay

Salina

Ally Land

Colliers

Colliers Point

A 4

The Mountain

Great Beach

Colliers Cay

A 3

★ Queen Elizabeth II Botanic Park

Sand Bluff

Sand Bluff

Frank Sound

Long Bridge

Gun Bay

CENTRAL

Blakes

Sparrowhawk Point

MANGROVE

A 4

SWAMP

A 3

Midland Acres

East End (Old Isaak's)

East Point

Breaker Point

Betty Bay Point

Frank Sound

Half Moon Bay

High Rock

se Bay

A 3

Cottage Point

Ironshore Point

Fragiles Flat

Ireland Bluff

DEWOOD BLIC BEACH

CARIBBEAN SEA

Orientation

With three separate and uniquely different islands to choose from, a
tour of the Cayman Islands nearly always means several days spent
in Grand Cayman, and then an excursion of another two or three
days to either Cayman Brac or Little Cayman.

Lying south of Miami and Cuba, and northwest of Jamaica, the islands
have a history inextricably linked to Britain. Today there is still a hint of
Britishness about these tropical isles that steadfastly remain a British territory.

Aside from the fantastic dive sites that can be found around all three of
the islands, Grand Cayman is where you will find a plethora of first-class
hotels and resorts, fine restaurants, sizzling nightlife, duty-free shopping
centers, and historic attractions. It is also the island that attracts the majority
of visitors, including thousands of cruise-ship passengers who debark in
the capital, George Town, each day. The largest of the three islands, Grand
Cayman is 28 miles (45km) long and 7 miles (11km) wide, with a population
of about 42,500. Excellent roads throughout the island make touring the
sites easy with either a rental car or taxi *(see pages 84–85)*. Explore George
Town's National Museum, shops and art galleries, bask on stunning Seven
Mile Beach, or enjoy nature's bountiful mangrove in the interior.

If you really want to spend your time on deserted beaches and intentionally
disconnect from the hustle and bustle of the modern world, Cayman
Brac or Little Cayman (89 miles/143km and 74 miles/120km northeast of Grand Cayman respectively and accessed by plane from
George Town) are the islands to visit for a peaceful interlude and
a back-to-nature experience. Your most likely companions on these
islands will be iguanas, exotic birds, an array of marine life,
and very few humans.

Planning your Visit

For an ideal Cayman Islands vacation it is suggested
that you pick from the nine tours listed in the Grand
Cayman section and find the choices that suit your
interests – sites of historic significance, botanical gardens and nature trails, submarine trips, scuba diving and
snorkeling, or visiting an interesting little town called
Hell. Then, decide on which of the two 'sister'
islands – Cayman Brac or Little Cayman – you
would like to see and plan an additional excursion around it.

Left: vividly-colored coral
Right: the pace of life is slow on the sister islands

Grand Cayman

1. A GEORGE TOWN WALKABOUT   *(see map below)*

A leisurely walk through downtown George Town with visits to the remains
of Fort George, the Elmslie United Memorial Church, the Cayman Islands
National Museum, and the wall of history at Quincentennial Square.
The walk can be completed in two to three hours, and is best done early
in the morning before the afternoon traffic jams cause gridlock.

*Comfortable shoes, sunscreen and a sunhat are suggested. You can also
check in advance with the tourist board to find out the cruise-ship sched-
ule and plan your tour to avoid the rush.*

Small, compact, and easy to explore on foot, the capital city of George Town
makes for a very pleasant morning walk. Although it is dense with banks and
insurance companies, it also has important historic sites and attractive old
buildings with architectural styles that include Victorian, Georgian, Colonial, and West Indian. There are numerous stores, cafés, and restaurants.

With the original name of Hogsties (wild boar were penned here to pro-
vide food for the crews of passing ships in the 17th century), the name of
George Town came about in the late 1700s and was created to honor Britain's
King George III. Free, historic walking-tour maps published by the National
Trust for the Cayman Islands (tel: 949 0121) are usually available at the
Trust House on Courts Road, off Eastern Avenue, and provide helpful infor-
mation for a self-guiding tour. The National Trust headquarters has been

George Town

150 m / 155 yds

····· Itinerary 1

Fort George (ruins) ★
Seaman's Memorial
Submarine Tours
Port Facility
George Town Harbour
Hog Sty Bay
Miss Eden Bay
Boiler's Rd
North Church Street
Government Building
Assembly Building
Fort Street
Church Hall
Panton Place
Elmslie United Memorial Church
HM Customs
South Church Street
Goring Ave
Walkers Road
Arch Road
Albert Panton Street
Court House
Edward Street
Cardinal Avenue
Post Office
Craft Market
Shedden Rd
Cayman Islands National Museum
Peace Memorial (Town Hall)
Clock Tower
Public Library

temporarily relocated to Webster
House (across the street from
Sunset House) at 359 South Church
Street following Hurricane Ivan in
2004. There is no telephone or
internet connection but visitors are
welcome.

Most of the action in downtown
George Town takes place near the
harbor, and a logical place to begin
a walking tour is at **Fort George**
on Harbour Drive near Fort Street.
Although it's right on the waterfront,
the fort is easy to miss since there
isn't very much of it left. Built in
1790 as a defense against Spanish
invaders from nearby Cuba, the
original fort was oval-shaped and
made of solid coral rock with walls
5ft (1.5m) thick. It wasn't as large

as most other forts in the Caribbean, but it was strategically located to ward off attacks. During World War II it was used by the Cayman Islands Home Guard (the local militia) as a guard tower to watch for the German submarines that often patrolled the Caribbean. To make way for new construction in the area, a real-estate developer demolished the fort in 1972, much to the chagrin of local historians who staged a protest on the waterfront. In 1987 the remains were deeded to the National Trust, which

then conducted an archeological dig that retrieved dozens of priceless artifacts that are now displayed in the Cayman Islands National Museum. Today, all that remains are three small portions of the wall and two long cannons. Near the fort is the **Seaman's Memorial**, which pays tribute to the islands' long seafaring history, and lists the names of 153 Caymanians who lost their lives at sea.

Cayman's Cathedral

Continuing south on Harbour Drive, you will come to two cruise-ship terminals, the **North Terminal** and the **South Terminal**. Almost identical, they handle several hundred thousand passengers each year who debark at this spot for tours of the island. They both have public washrooms that are always kept neat and clean. Across the street from the terminals on Harbour Drive is the **Elmslie United Memorial Church** (Mon–Fri 9am–5pm, with services on Sunday at 9.30am and 11am; tel: 949 7923). Named for one of the first Presbyterian ministers in Grand Cayman, who served on the island from 1846 to 1863, and built in 1920 by shipbuilder Captain Rayal Bodden, the church is an impressive structure with a timber roof shaped like an upturned

schooner hull. Constructed on the site of the original church that dated from 1835, it is often called 'Cayman's very own cathedral.' During the 1860s, the Elmslie Church group established six other churches on the island.

This church was the first building in the Cayman Islands constructed out of concrete blocks, and Captain Bodden visited Jamaica beforehand to learn how to make the concrete

Top: the simple exterior of the Elmslie Church
Above: the *George Town Galleon* sets sail

molds. Inside, the sleek mahogany pews were crafted by another local ship-builder, and the ceiling was made from wood salvaged from old sailing ships. The bold-colored stained-glass windows were donated by Dr Roy McTaggert, a local man often credited with persuading Caymanians to retain British colony status. Recently restored to its original condition, it also contains several memorial plaques and old, stone grave markers shaped like small houses. Set amid the bright and noisy commercial district, it offers a cool and contemplative respite from the relentless hot sun.

The National Museum

Farther along Harbour Drive, past gleaming duty-free stores, you will spot an island-style white building with a bright red roof and a flagpole out front. This is the **Cayman Islands National Museum**, a treasure chest that serves as the Cayman Islands collective memory and link to the past. It is closed while undergoing major refurbishment following extensive damage caused by Hurricane Ivan, but the museum shop remains open (Mon–Fri 9am–5pm, Sat 10am–2pm). One of the finest museums in the Caribbean, it is one of the more popular attractions in the city. The museum got its start in the 1950s when a local man named Ira Thompson started collecting 'odds and ends' of Caymanian history. A professional driver by trade, Thompson's collection grew so large that he opened the Cayman Museum in a small building on South Church Street. For his dedication to island history, Thompson was awarded a Certificate of Honor by Elizabeth II of Britain, and eventually he donated all his artifacts to the government, which later created the Cayman Islands National Museum.

Housed in the city's Old Courthouse, which dates to the 1830s, it is the second-oldest surviving building in Grand Cayman and a classic example of a Caymanian 'upstairs house.' The first floor is

Top: the Cayman Islands National Museum, one of the finest in the Caribbean. **Right:** a little boy with a serious view on life constructed of wattle and daub, and the second floor – complete with verandah – is made of framed timber. Green wooden hurricane shutters adorn the windows. It once had a large lantern on top that helped sailors of the day to navigate the port. Through the years, the building has played many roles, including parsonage, court house, post office, library, and jail. The dozen steps that lead to the top floor, which once housed the court room, brought the local expression 'walking the twelve steps' into being, which means that you are about to pay the price for your bad deeds.

Inside is a stunning array of over 2,000 artifacts that draw on the history of the islands. Near the entrance is an air-conditioned theater that runs a continuous 10-minute audiovisual display on Caymanian culture and history. Departing the theater, you walk through a display that depicts each stage of the traditional building technique known as wattle and daub. Around the corner you come to the **Natural History Exhibit** with a three-dimensional depiction of the undersea mountains and canyons offshore, including an excellent diagram explaining the Cayman Trench. It also has educational displays of dry woodlands, beach sand, swamps, shells, caymanite, and indigenous plants and trees. Nearby is a submarine's porthole that contains a fish tank with moray eels and tropical fish. The museum's **Cultural History Gallery** hosts rotating exhibits that focus on the people of the Cayman Islands. Other rooms contain a collection of furniture made by Wilbanks Miller, a highly regarded ship's carpenter who was born in 1881, as well as tools, cooking utensils, sisal switches used to swat mosquitos, and thick leather sandals, commonly called 'wompers,' that were worn by early settlers.

Maritime Heritage Trail

You can learn more about the seafaring history of the islands on the maritime heritage trail, which explores sites across Grand Cayman, Little Cayman, and Cayman Brac.

In Grand Cayman visitors can follow a driving route through West Bay, downtown George Town, and the northeast side of the island. Definitely worth a visit is **Pull-and-be-Damned Point** in South Sound. This is the offshore site of the wreck *Pallas*, an 1875 Norwegian ship that was blown off course and swept onto the reef that lies south of George Town. Fragments of iron from the wreckage can still be seen poking out of the water. A map of the trail is available at the National Museum or from the National Trust.

Shopping and Exploring

On the downtown streets there are art galleries, restaurants, and outdoor cafés. And, of course, the world-famous duty-free shopping centers that attract thousands of cruise-ship passengers each day with their dazzling displays of discount gold watches, designer clothing, perfumes, cosmetics, luggage, crystal, electronics, liquor, leather goods, diamond and emerald jewelry, and hand-rolled premium Cuban cigars.

Right: getting ready for an underwater adventure

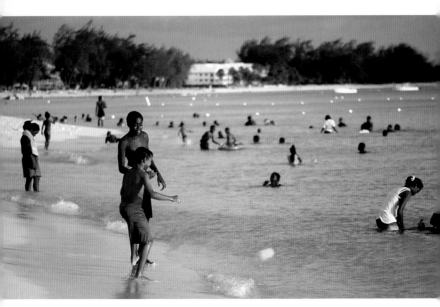

Other points of interest in the downtown area include the **Cayman Islands National Archives** (Mon–Fri 8.30am–5pm; free; tel: 949 9809), off Crewe Road near Thomas Russell Way, which is full of historic materials, such as births and deaths records from the 19th century. Cardinal Avenue in the heart of George Town has some major names in duty-free shopping. Close by is the **Craft Market**, a favorite stop for tourists shopping for island-made souvenirs.

At the intersection of Fort and Edward streets is the **Clock Tower**. Built in 1937 in honor of King George V, the tower is just one of many monuments in the city that characterize the Caymanian allegiance to Great Britain. Opposite the Clock Tower is the **Peace Memorial**, built in 1919, which served as the Town Hall for many years and was the center of life in the city, hosting everything from community dances to important political meetings. It was in this building that the Cayman Islands officially voted to forgo independence in 1962. It is most noted, however, for the fact that it was dedicated in the name of peace rather than war. Across from the clock is **Quincentennial Square**, an area refurbished in 2003 to celebrate Cayman's 500th anniversary. Here is a five-panel mural, the **Wall of History**, created to commemorate the people and events that shaped the islands.

Also on Edward Street is the **Public Library**, erected in 1939 and well stocked with books on Cayman Islands history and culture. Built by Captain Bodden, who was also responsible for the Elmslie Church on Harbour Drive, the library has a timbered ceiling decorated with ornate shields from many of the finest universities in Great Britain. The contents of the library are temporarily housed at the Commerce Building on Dr Roy's Drive, around the corner from the original building. Directly behind the library is an area of the city that was used by the US Navy during World War II. Here, while conducting social functions and filming news reports, several US officers met and fell in love with Caymanian women who became known as island war brides.

Above: room to play on Seven Mile Beach

2. SEVEN MILE BEACH/WEST BAY/HELL   *(see map, p28)*

Venture up the glorious coast of Seven Mile Beach, mail the requisite postcards from Hell, and visit the world-renowned Cayman Turtle Farm.

Grand Cayman's **Seven Mile Beach** prides itself on being a self-contained vacation paradise where visitors can find everything they need. This highly developed stretch of white, sandy beach is jam-packed with hotels, condominiums, restaurants, bars, stores, and water-sports operators, and is the nucleus of the island's tourism industry. It is also congested.

Sandwiched between the North Sound and the sea, Seven Mile Beach begins at the northern outskirts of George Town and is 6 miles (10km) long. There is commercial development from the north to the West Bay district and along the way is the Ritz-Carlton hotel the island's tallest, and largest resort, towering above its neighbors. The beach itself is stunning, with clear, calm water that is ideal for swimming.

Start your trek up Seven Mile Beach at **The Butterfly Farm** (Mon–Sat 8.30am–4pm, Sun 8.30–noon; admission fee; tel: 946 3411), a tranquil oasis under mesh that contains landscaped gardens and ponds stocked with Japanese fish. Hundreds of butterflies from all over the world fly freely. There is an informative guided tour, and visitors are given a complimentary return ticket. The farm shop stocks butterfly-related souvenirs.

To the north of Seven Mile Beach the road enters **West Bay**, the second-largest district in Grand Cayman, with a population of about 8,000. Here, the name of the main thoroughfare changes to North West Point Road and the atmosphere becomes more residential. First settled in the 1740s, West Bay was once a community of turtle hunters and mariners. A century or so later, substantial phosphate deposits led to the development of a mining industry, and by the 1780s this was the main source of income in the area. However, in the early 1900s better-quality deposits were discovered in Florida and the industry here went bust.

Inland, West Bay is graced with cow pastures, schools, soccer fields, and churches. The **West Bay United Church** (usually open during daylight hours; services Sunday 9am and 7pm) is especially interesting. It was designed to resemble a classic Caymanian sailing ship and has a pulpit made of local mahogany, as well as stunning stained-glass windows.

Local Insights

Continuing north, the road comes to one of the few stop-lights in the area and a tiny building in a little shopping center, the **Powell's Heritage Museum** (Mon–Thur 10am–5pm; admission fee; tel: 949 3477). The passion of a native Caymanian, Tony Powell, this hot and dusty, privately owned museum is housed in an old general store and is filled with farming tools, books, letters, maps, prayer books, school report cards, photographs, fishing

Above: the Devil's Hangout is picture perfect kitsch

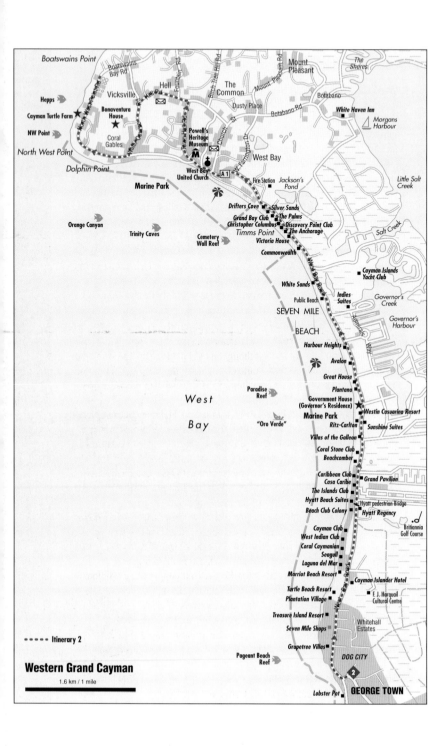

Boatswains Point

Boatswains
Bay Rd

Hell

The
Common

Mount
Pleasant

The
Shores

Hepps

Vicksville

Cayman Turtle Farm

Bonaventura
House

NW Point

Coral
Gables

North West Point

Dolphin Point

Marine Park

Orange Canyon

Trinity Caves

Cemetery
Wall Reef

Powell's
Heritage
Museum

West Bay
United Church

Dusty Place

Botabano

White Haven Inn

Morgans
Harbour

West Bay

Fire Station

Jackson's
Pond

Little Salt
Creek

Drifters Cove

Silver Sands

Grand Bay Club

The Palms

Christopher Columbus

Discovery Point Club

Timms Point

The Anchorage

Victoria House

Commonwealth

White Sands

Public Beach

SEVEN MILE

BEACH

Salt Creek

Cayman Islands
Yacht Club

Indies
Suites

Governor's
Creek

Governor's
Harbour

Harbour Heights

Avalon

Great House

West
Bay

Paradise
Reef

"Oro Verde"

Plantana

Government House
(Governor's Residence)

Marine Park

Ritz-Carlton

Villas of the Galleon

Coral Stone Club

Beachcomber

Caribbean Club

Casa Caribe

The Islands Club

Hyatt Beach Suites

Beach Club Colony

Westin Casuarina Resort

Sunshine Suites

Grand Pavilion

Hyatt pedestrian Bridge

Hyatt Regency

Britannia
Golf Course

Cayman Club

West Indian Club

Coral Caymanian

Seagull

Laguna del Mar

Marriot Beach Resort

Turtle Beach Resort

Plantation Village

Treasure Island Resort

Seven Mile Shops

Grapetree Villas

Pageant Beach
Reef

Cayman Islander Hotel

F. J. Harquail
Cultural Centre

Whitehall
Estates

DOG CITY

2

Lobster Pot

GEORGE TOWN

----- Itinerary 2

Western Grand Cayman

1.6 km / 1 mile

equipment, sewing machines, and old documents; wandering around the museum feels like making a visit to grandma's house.

To Hell and Back

Just beyond the stop-light, the road forks and a rusty white sign with an arrow pointing to **Hell** appears. This area is a maze of tiny back roads, and many people joke that they never thought they'd have a hard time going to Hell. After driving about half a mile (1km) along this road (which has no name), you will spot another sign that says Hell Road and you will see the fleet of tour buses that cart about 500 cruise-ship passengers here every day. Although it is easily classified as a tourist trap, Hell is a cheerful place.

Full of kitsch and kick, the so-called town consists of a gas station, post office, and about six gift shops. One of those shops, the **Devil's Hangout** (daily 7am–5pm; tel: 949 1087), is on everyone's itinerary. As visitors walk in the door, owner Ivan Farrington greets them with his standard repertoire: 'Welcome to the coolest place in Hell.' 'How the hell are you?' 'Where the hell are you from?' 'What the hell do you want?'

Usually dressed in a frilly tuxedo shirt, black bow tie, red cape, and red horns, Farrington is a Caymanian who has lived on Hell Road since he was a child. A local legend who has become a media darling, he's a natural performer, whose business card says: 'For a date with the Devil call Ivan Farrington.'

The shelves here are stocked with Hot-as-Hell pepper sauce, diplomas from the University of Hell, and cups, plates and spoons emblazoned with fiery Hell logos. And, of course, souvenir T-shirts that say: 'Been to Hell and Back,' and 'Never Tell Your Mother to go to Hell Because She'll Buy You One of these Stupid Shirts and Make You Wear it to School.'

Bleak, Black Rocks

In the early 1930s, Commissioner Cardinal from Britain was visiting the West Bay District and decided to do some bird hunting. Rifle in hand, he aimed for

Top: an observation deck overlooks the stark, black rocks of Hell
Right: even in Hell, you mustn't drop litter

a lone heron sitting amid a vast field of stark, grayish, blackish rocks, and said, 'This place looks like Hell.' The name stuck; the commissioner missed his shot. The bleak and desolate rocks that caught the commissioner's eye do look like the charred remains of an inferno, and are the main attraction of a visit to Hell. A winding wooden walkway that stretches out behind the gift shops leads to an observation deck that overlooks acres of pinnacles and ridges. A black statue of the devil stands guard, perhaps to reinforce the numerous signs sternly warning visitors that 'The Removal of Hell Rocks is Prohibited.'

The brittle, pockmarked rocks are over a million years old, and are the result of a chemical reaction involving limestone, calcium, and magnesium. They were then transformed even more by thousands of years of interaction with brackish water and pockets of algae. More commonly known as dolomite, in the Cayman Islands this porous, sedimentary rock is called iron-shore. The official scientific name is phytokarst. The prefix – phyto – means plant, and the suffix – karst – means eroded landform. At the base of the rocks are shallow pools of water full of schools of minnows.

This bleak landscape evokes a hauntingly eerie, Dante-esque mood. The rocks' pinnacles are so sharp they're almost impossible to walk on. While growing up island children are told ghost stories about evil spirits that inhabit the rocks, and teenage couples (prepared to brave the demons) often come here late at night in search of privacy. Every now and then, especially at Christmas, local people float a coat of oil on the water and set the rocks on fire, which is a sight to behold.

Many people who come here can't resist mailing a postcard from Hell to friends and family back home. The **Hell Post Office** (Mon–Fri 8.30am–5pm; tel: 949 1171) is a modern little facility well equipped to handle the hordes of tourists who come in.

Above: the Cayman Turtle Farm plays a serious environmental role

Turtle Time

After leaving Hell and getting back to North Bay Road, continue northward and in less than a mile (1.5km) you will find the **Cayman Turtle Farm** (daily 8.30am–5pm; admission fee; tel: 949 3894). One of the most-visited places in the Cayman Islands, and the only one of its kind in the world, the farm is much more than a tourist attraction, and soon to become part of a massive marine and nature park *(for details, see page 32)*. Rooted deep in the Cayman culture, the turtle represented a way of life and livelihood that today has almost disappeared. Now an endangered species, the green sea turtles were on their way to extinction in the islands until the Turtle Farm came to the rescue.

Founded in 1968 to breed and raise turtles commercially, the farm has successfully implemented a breed-and-release program that has returned over 30,000 tagged turtles to the wild. Many of them return to Cayman Island beaches to nest their eggs, and they are often spotted by divers offshore. Others have been seen as far away as Venezuela, Nicaragua, Panama, and Mexico.

Each year the farm produces on average 10,000 hatchlings. The mating season occurs between April and July, with eggs being laid a few months later. Females usually lay five to seven clutches, each containing approximately 100 eggs. The eggs at the farm are collected at the time of laying and transferred to incubators, where the temperature is maintained at 82°F (26.6°C). The temperature determines the sex of the turtle, and this temperature control ensures an equal number of males and females hatched. If the temperature drops just a few degrees, the result is all male turtles. If it's any warmer, it means all females. Each egg takes 60 days to hatch, and then the fragile babies are transferred to sand boxes for a few days before being placed in water again. Weighing only a few ounces, the babies are fed a special diet that enables them to grow to about 8–10ins (20–25cm) long and weigh 6lbs (2.7kg) in one year.

The farm is a land-based operation and the turtles are raised in enormous tanks filled with seawater that is pumped in fresh every day. Visitors are awestruck by the sight of over 16,000 turtles gracefully swimming around with their heads bobbing and flippers flapping. A concrete walkway takes visitors past the tanks that each contain turtles of the same size. Ranging from the cute little babies to fully mature ones weighing in at 600lbs (272kg), the creatures appear strong and healthy and not at all bothered by the fact that they are held in captivity. There is a sandy, man-made beach where females are placed to lay their eggs.

Exact feeding times vary, but as a rough guide the turtles are fed early in the morning and again late in the afternoon, and the commotion in the water when this takes place is thrilling. While visitors are asked not to touch or feed them, many of the turtles are

Right: feeding time for the turtles

quite friendly and swim right up to people leaning over the tanks. The farm has tanks with young turtles that can be touched, with supervision – a perfect photo opportunity.

In addition to the turtles released into the wild, quite a large number of them wind up as delicacies on the menus of island restaurants. Turtle meat has for centuries been a dietary staple of the Caymanian community, and environmentalists believe that satisfying the local demand for turtle meat in this way eliminates the need to hunt the creatures in the wild, and is in the long run good for the turtle population.

The farm is a major research center and scientists from universities throughout the world come here to conduct studies on the social behavior, aging, stress, and population dynamics of the species. It also does valuable conservation work by educating the tens of thousands of visitors who come here each year. Although the turtles are, of course, the main event, there are also several other indigenous animals on display, such as Cayman green parrots, rock iguanas, crocodiles, and agouti (an indigenous species rather like a small rabbit). The large gift shop stocks a wide selection of turtle and marine-inspired gifts and souvenirs.

The Turtle Farm is to be part of a $42-million theme park called Boatswain's (pronounced Bo-sun's) Beach. Opening in 2006, the park will allow guests to swim and snorkel with turtles, fish, and other marine life in the saltwater lagoon. There will also be a predator's tank that you can view from the lagoon, and a bird aviary. The operational area of the existing Turtle Farm is approximately 4 acres (1.6 hectares); however, the entire Boatswain Beach project is over seven times larger at 30 acres (12 hectares).

3. STINGRAY CITY *(see map, p18)*

A trek to Stingray City, considered one of the world's top dive sites, to snorkel and feed the stingrays. While it's a delightful thing to do, snorkeling in Stingray City can be an intense experience for first-timers.

Wearing a T-shirt and sunblock lotion while in the water is advised. Several operators offer tours to Stingray City that include snorkeling gear, drinks, and snacks, as well as the boat ride. Prices range from US$25–50 per person. Depending on how many stops the boats make, the tours last from four to six hours.

Top of the list of things to do in Grand Cayman must be an excursion to Stingray City. To miss it would be a bit like visiting Rome and not taking in the Colosseum. It's something you've just got to do – and if you don't, you'll regret it.

Right: stingrays should only be touched with bare hands, to protect their skin

Located in the North Sound, between West Bay and Rum Point, Stingray City is often called the best 12-ft (3.5-meter) dive in the world. It consists of two distinct spots – **Stingray City** itself, and the **Sandbar** – two shallow, sheltered areas in calm, clear waters, with coral heads, a barrier reef, and literally hundreds of the curious stingrays.

Both Stingray City and the Sandbar have been featured in *National Geographic* magazine as among the most spectacular dive locations in the world. At Stingray City, snorkelers swim round a sandbar while the rays play in the water around them. At the Sandbar, the water is so shallow that you can actually stand up and wade through it while dozens of rays swim around your feet, so it is ideal for children and non-swimmers.

The reason there are so many stingrays in the vicinity is that, many years ago, local fishermen used to come here to clean their catch before bringing it ashore, and they would dump the unwanted remains in the water. After a while, the stingrays just naturally began congregating in the area, knowing that they could expect an easy meal.

For Novices and Experts Alike

Although boat-loads of visitors now come here each day to share this unusual experience, it remains a prominent dive site and even 'serious' divers still like to use it. While some visitors come equipped with full scuba gear, most find that just a mask and snorkel is all they need. In fact, people who don't even know how to swim are able to take in the Stingray City experience. After decades as a tourist attraction, the rays have grown accustomed to all the action and usually swoop in and swarm around the boats as soon as they arrive. Ranging in size from 2ft to 5ft (60cm to 1.5m) wide, they are not at all shy about accepting a free meal and will either bump into you or rub up against your body if they sense you have food and are holding out on them. They will also glide right by you flapping their 'wings' as a signal, in case you had failed to notice them. Every now and then some nosy fish (usually groupers or snappers) will come by, trying to get a piece of the action. The food – which is usually tidbits of raw squid – is brought to the site by the dive masters and then doled out by hand.

Above: stingrays swoop and swarm around boats and curious visitors

Southern Atlantic stingrays – their proper name is *Dasyatis Americana* – don't bite, but they do have sharp pointers on their tails that can sting a person's skin quite seriously, hence their name. As they pass by, you can reach out and touch their velvety undersides and they won't be perturbed. But, as the dive masters will warn you, you should touch them only with your bare hands, because diving gloves can remove the protective mucous that coats their skin.

It is a great experience to feed the creatures yourself but be prepared for the feeding frenzy that churns the water when you do so. And remember to hold the palm of your hand out flat with the food on it, as if you were feeding a horse, so that the rays don't nip your skin by mistake.

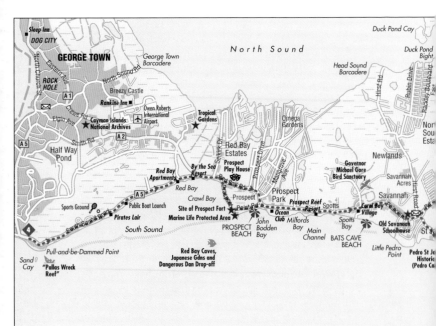

Above: the Pedro St James Historic Site, a magnificently restored building

4. THE SOUTHEAST COAST *(see map, p34–5)*

A glimpse of the historic side of Grand Cayman with a ride along the Southeast Coast, taking in Prospect, Savanna, Pedro St James Historic Site, and Bodden Town.

Just a few miles east of George Town, Grand Cayman has several interesting spots where the history of the islands comes vividly to life. Heading east from the capital along South Sound Road, past the luxury homes and sprawling estates that line the waterfront here (sadly, many of which were extensively damaged by Hurricane Ivan), the highway turns into Red Bay Road and continues through **Prospect**. Although all that is left to mark its historic significance is a small, hard-to-find monument, Prospect was once the site of a massive, 18th-century fort that was built to defend the island from pirates. In 1846, a terrible hurricane wiped out the fort and most of the houses and buildings in the surrounding area.

Nearby is the **Watler Cemetery**, a family burial ground that contains the remains of the Watler family, who were among the earliest settlers on the island, back in the early 1700s. Their descendants donated this land to the National Trust for the Cayman Islands in 1991, to be turned into an historic monument. Open to the public, the cemetery is surrounded by an old stone wall and has dozens of graves with well-maintained tombstones decorated with coral rocks and seashells.

A few miles past the cemetery is the town of **Savannah**. The first building of significance here is the **Old Savannah Schoolhouse**, built in 1940 and recently restored by the National Trust. Surrounded by a garden of pink, pur-

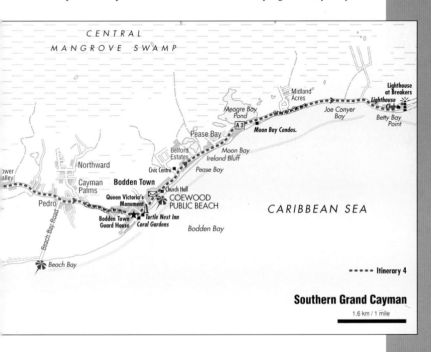

Southern Grand Cayman

1.6 km / 1 mile

ple, and white periwinkle flowers, the one-room schoolhouse closed in 1981 when a more modern school was built nearby, but it remains as a reminder of days gone by.

Pedro St James

The major attraction of Savannah, and the most important historic site on the entire island, is **Pedro St James Historic Site** (daily 9am–5pm; admission fee; tel: 947 3329). Also known as Pedro Castle, this magnificently-restored great house is considered by local people to be the birthplace of democracy in the Cay-

man Islands. Signs on the highway clearly mark the turn-off point that leads down a bumpy street to the site entrance. Once inside the property, guests pass through the impressive Visitors' Centre and gift shop with a modern, air-conditioned restaurant right next door. Close to the Visitors' Centre is a comfortable theater that runs a continuous, state-of-the-art, 24-minute multimedia presentation depicting the role Pedro St James played in Caymanian history.

Perched on a limestone cliff with panoramic views of Old Jones Bay and surrounded by formal English gardens, the great house at St James was originally built by William Eden from Wiltshire in England in 1780 and is the oldest stone structure still standing in Grand Cayman. Sturdy and well built, it has survived the numerous hurricanes that have wiped out most other historic structures on the island. Lush green lawns dotted with palms and flowering plants flow down from the house, and there's a walk around the peaceful 7-acre (2.8-ha) property that offers a realistic view of what colonial life was like hundreds of years ago.

Constructed by slave labor, the three-story main house is made of native stone with outer walls 3ft (1m) thick, and dark-green wooden louvers on every window for protection from the weather. It is a classic manor-type house with a gabled roof and outside staircase. On the first floor there is a large kitchen adjoined by two smaller rooms, one of which was sometimes used as a jail cell to hold criminals before they were shipped off to Jamaica for trial.

The second floor houses the formal dining room surrounded by wrap-around verandahs, and the bedrooms and sitting room are on the third floor. Restored to their original condition, all the rooms are furnished with period antiques and artifacts, including mahogany tables, rocking chairs, four-poster beds, earthenware storage jars, silverware, wrought-iron candelabras, cooking utensils, old photographs, linens, and lace curtains.

It was at Pedro St James in 1831 that local citizens gathered to plot their future and formalize plans to hold elections on the island. Prior to this date most deci-

Top: a welcoming sign outside the Pedro St James Historic Site
Above: small children pose for a picture

sions concerning life and politics in the Cayman Islands were made by the governor of Jamaica. Less than a week after that crucial meeting, the first Legislative Assembly for the Cayman Islands was elected. In 1835, the Declaration of Emancipation freeing local slaves was read from the front steps of the house. But in 1877 tragedy struck when one of the daughters of the house was killed by a bolt of lightning. So grief-stricken were the rest of the family that they chose to move out of their home, and it sat vacant for the next 100 years. In 1991 the Cayman Islands Government purchased the house and surrounding property, declaring it a national landmark. They began a restoration process that cost over US$7 million and took more than seven years to complete.

Pedro St James was badly damaged by Hurricane Ivan and is currently undergoing major refurbishment.

Bodden Town

Back out on the highway, the road passes through **Newlands**, where pastures grazed by cattle and goats dot the landscape. About 3 miles (5km) farther to the east it eases into **Bodden Town**. Once the capital city of the Cayman Islands, Bodden Town is rich in history and has a number of compelling sites. Unfortunately many coastal properties in Bodden Town were severely damaged by Hurricane Ivan. The town is said to have had one of the first wells ever dug on the island and was the main source of potable water for many early settlers. It was first developed by the oldest family in the Cayman Islands, the Bodden clan, and was originally called South Side. In 1773, a map-maker started using the new name because of the number of families called Bodden he found residing in the area. In 1800 the town was a bustling community with 375 residents, but soon afterward it slipped to second-class status when development started in George Town.

The earliest and the most prominent of the Boddens was William Bodden, who served as the chief magistrate and as major general of the island's militia from 1798 until his death in 1823. Bodden was fondly called the Grand Old Man of Grand Cayman and is remembered for being instrumental in the building of the first roads, churches, and large schooners in Grand Cayman. Bodden is, in fact, the most common surname on the island, and in only a few days here you are bound to bump into someone who shares it. It is also the name of the district that includes Savannah and other nearby towns.

Paying tribute to British history, the first attraction of note is **Queen Victoria's Monument**. Built in 1910 by the residents of Bodden Town, in honor of the late queen, the monument was often

Right: an island idyll – a seat in the shade on a sandy shore used during the 1920s and 1930s for open-air community meetings of local men who congregated here to discuss politics, sport, and island news. Not far away are **Guard House Park** and **Gun Square**. With an adjacent parking lot, the Guard House was originally built for protection against pirates and the Spanish marauders who often tried to invade the island from the nearby shore. It also provided shelter for the military men who watched over the area. What remains of the original house is an old stone wall, a memorial plaque with historic information about the site, and two cannons that point in the direction of the sea. Nearby Gun Square used to be the site of a small

but strategically important British fort that guarded the town.

A short walk eastward from Gun Square is **Meagre Bay Pond**, which was used in the early 1900s as a hunting area by local people who came here to shoot duck and teal. These days it's a popular bird-watching spot and nature sanctuary because hunting in the area is now illegal and many migratory waterfowl have begun using it as a base. Early in the morning and late in the afternoon, people come here to watch the hundreds of herons, egrets, cormorants, ibis, stilts, teals, and willets that gather to feed.

Situated behind the Gun Square, **Mission House** is another historic building in the Bodden district. Built in the 1840s by slave labor, Mission House is a classic wattle and daub structure that was used by Christian missionaries to the islands. Last on the list of echoes from the past in the town is the **Slave Wall**. It can be found at the end of Old Monument Road and is marked by a small historic sign. Sometimes referred to as Drummond's Wall, named in memory of the slave who supervised its construction, this old stone wall was built some time in the early 1800s for protection from attackers, and was

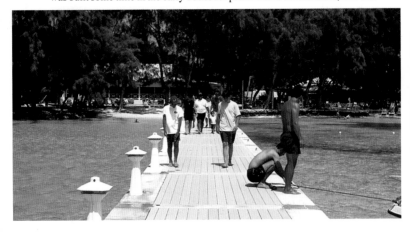

Top: enjoying a cool drink with daddy
Above: on one of the walkways at Rum Point

originally several miles long. A few sections of it remain intact, but most of it has been worn down by storms or ravaged by scavengers who stole the valuable stones to build their own homes nearby.

A Perfect End

The perfect way to end a day trip along the southeast coast is to stop for dinner at the **Lighthouse Restaurant** (tel: 947 2047), just a few miles east of Bodden Town in an area called Breakers. The Lighthouse is a local landmark, with elegant indoor seating along with a dining space on a verandah that hangs right out over the sea. The sound of waves crashing onto the shore mingles with the strains of the classical music that is played in the background. Decorated with nautical artifacts and photos of striking lighthouses from around the world, the restaurant serves Italian and seafood specialties such as shrimp and lobster sautéed in olive oil, pesto focaccia bread with shaved parmesan cheese, thick lasagnes, wood-roasted salmon, and an assortment of Italian pastries and cheesecakes. The Lighthouse Restaurant underwent major refurbishments after it was badly damaged by Hurricane Ivan.

5. NORTH SIDE *(see map, p40)*

A drive through the laid-back residential neighborhood of North Side, on the North Shore, with stops at Caribbean Charlie's, Rum Point, Cayman Kai, and Booby Cay.

Although there is a convenient ferry that takes passengers from the Seven Mile Beach area to Rum Point in North Side, the long drive that begins in George Town is worth the effort. If you come by car you have the option of tooling around the various neighborhoods once you arrive, rather than being stranded in one spot. And slowly winding past the string of funky beach houses that line the North Shore, you get an immediate sense of a casual community where the vehicles of choice are beat-up old jeeps rather than modern, air-conditioned sedans. Lacking the razzle-dazzle of more highly-developed tourist areas nearer George Town, this area of Grand Cayman is far more mellow, down-to-earth, and easy to enjoy.

Departing from downtown George Town, drive east on South Sound Road until it turns in to Red Bay Road, and continue east along the coast until you get to Frank Sound. Here, turn left onto Frank Sound Road, the only road that dissects the island. Continue along this road, past Queen Elizabeth II Botanic Park, several cow pastures, and not much else until it ends on the northern coast. Once here, you can take off in either direction and explore the most secluded and least populated part of Grand Cayman. Many of the homes here have jokey names hanging on signs out front – *Time Out, No Big Ting, Paradise Found, Ho Hum, Happy to be Home.*

Right: a sleek yacht in the waters of Cayman Kai

Caribbean Charlie

Just a few miles west of Queen's Highway on North Side Road, a tiny wooden signpost that is easy to miss points the way to **Caribbean Charlie's** (tel: 947 9453). After winding down a bumpy dirt road, you reach the inland neighborhood officially known as **Hutland**. It is said to have got its name from the numerous small huts that were built here by local farmers in the late 19th century. Smack in the middle of Hutland, and surrounded by fruit trees, a whimsical little cottage with gingerbread trim and a tropical garden comes into view and you know that you have arrived.

Charlie Ebanks and his wife, Elaine, are usually inside hard at work, but quickly appear to greet visitors. A native-born Caymanian artist still practicing a dying art form, Charlie has become world famous for his hand-made wooden birdcages that are often sold before they're even completed. Painted in bright colors – lizard green, shocking pink, Caribbean blue, sunburst yellow – the cages are each uniquely designed replicas of homes and historic buildings in the Cayman Islands, and come with a registration number and certificate of ownership.

Charlie travels away from the island several times a year to collect the wood he uses; types range from teak to mahogany and pine. Since the 1980s, fans of his work have been stopping by to add more and more pieces to their personal collections. Along with the cages, Charlie also produces custom-made furniture, wall plaques, towel racks, knick knacks, and warri boards, used for playing a

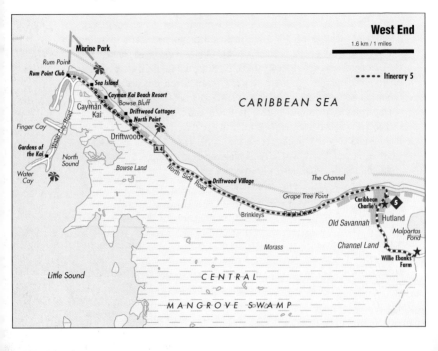

grand cayman

checkers-like game, which originated in Africa and today is common in the Caribbean. And each night at about sundown, Charlie and his New Jersey-born wife crank up the reggae, break out the rum, and start dancing in the middle of their shop. Just the chance to meet the two of them makes the drive to the West End well worthwhile.

Not far from Caribbean Charlie's, and also in Hutland, Willie Ebanks (Charlie's brother) runs a pig farm that oddly enough attracts many visitors, although it's not your average tourist destination. Along with tending to his hogs, Willie has taken it upon himself to protect and feed a large flock of West Indian whistling ducks that now call his property home. A protected species that was becoming more and more rare in the Cayman Islands, the whistling ducks are now abundant, thanks to Willie Ebanks. On a small pond behind his house, hundreds of these birds – they actually do whistle rather than quack – start congregating late in the afternoon and then line up, patiently waiting for Willie to bring them their evening meal.

Rum Point to Booby Cay

Heading farther west on North Side Road will take you right into **Rum Point**. Legend has it that back in the old pirate days, a ship loaded with hundreds of bottles of rum sank off-shore from this spot and that's how it got its name. A small peninsula of land that sits under a dense canopy of casuarina and Australian pine trees, Rum Point is a lively commercial enclave of sun decks and wooden walkways, with a restaurant, bar, gift shop, picnic tables, hammocks, and a broad, white beach that is popular with local families and young peo-ple. Visitors here take it easy, loll around in the sun, and just enjoy the view. Along with a very relaxed atmo-sphere, water-sports are the main draw here and several operators offer windsurf boards, hobie cats, small sailboats, bicycles, and snorkeling equip-ment for rent, as well as trips in glass-bottomed boats.

Just a bit to the south of Rum Point is **Cayman Kai**, a residential neighborhood of plush waterfront homes with million-dollar price tags, and the **Cayman Kai Beach Resort**. Kai means by the sea, and this entire area is enveloped in the salty scent of the ocean. Many people come here to bicycle, jog, or just stroll through the beautiful neighborhood.

A little farther to the south is **Booby Cay**, a protected bird sanctuary nestled inside **North Sound**. About 30 sq. miles (78 sq. km) in diameter, North Sound is a region of mangrove swamps and small mangrove islands that are ideal nesting spots for birds, especially the boobies that roost here year round. Other birds likely to be spotted include herons, egrets, ospreys,

Left: building castles in the sand
Above: take it easy at Cayman Kai

ducks, and frigates. It is also a favorite spot for kayakers who come to poke around the channels cut into the dense mangroves, and listen to the sounds of the birds. Only about 15ft (5m) deep, the waters of North Sound are crystal clear and almost always calm.

6. EAST END *(see map, p42)*

An afternoon drive to the East End of the island with visits to Goring Bluff Lighthouse, Gun Bay, and the Memorial to the Wreck of the Ten Sails.

East of Bodden Town and past Frank Sound, the coastal highway meanders through the district of **East End**, a delightful area of quiet beaches, wind-blown trees, busy fishing boats, quaint Caymanian cottages, and small, family-run stores. One of the prettiest beaches in this area is **Heritage Beach**, a small public area maintained by the National Trust. The oldest continuously settled community on the island, East End was founded in the late 17th century by Isaac Bodden, and the district is still sometimes referred to as **Old Isaac's**, its original name. Isaac was the grandson of William Bodden, one of the first settlers to make his home in Grand Cayman *(see page 37)*.

Kids will enjoy a run about in the Captain George Dixon Park at East End's quaint little village. One of five parks that are on the agenda for

Eastern Grand Cayman
1.6 km / 1 miles

development by the Dart family, the Captain George Dixon Park provides shady relief with its cabanas and lush vegetation as well as slides and climbing frames for little ones to enjoy.

A bit farther down the highway the **East End Lighthouse** appears, perched atop Goring Bluff. For centuries, there have been lighthouses on this part of the coast. One of the first was simply a large lantern hoisted up a 75-ft (23-m) ship's mast, followed by a more substantial one using a kerosene lamp, that was built in 1912. The coastal road didn't extend this far until 1935, and before that most people arrived here by boat. The current lighthouse, built in 1937, is solar-powered; it still functions as the main navigation marker for this end of the island. A few years ago the Cayman Islands National Trust built a pretty park around it, laid out with walkways, a flower garden, and an array of medicinal plants of the kind grown by early settlers.

Less than a mile from the Lighthouse is **Gun Bay**, a small town that was first settled in the 1800s. At the time, Gun Bay was one of two legal entry points to the Cayman Islands and the community that lived here was responsible for controlling the maritime traffic, trading with passing ships, and registering all the births, deaths, and marriages that took place in the East End.

A Maritime Disaster

The most significant thing about Gun Bay is that it was the site of the **Wreck of the Ten Sails**, and several monuments mark the spot of the most tragic maritime accident in Cayman Islands' history. A look-out point called **Queen's View** also stands by the shore, and a huge anchor that can be spotted jutting out of the water just offshore is said to have belonged to one of the sunken ships.

It was here, in the early morning hours of February 8, 1794, that 10 British merchant ships were swept off course by strong winds and thrust into the treacherous coral reef. Part of a convoy of 58 merchant vessels escorted by a British Navy frigate, HMS *Convert*, the ships had left Jamaica two days earlier and were en route for Britain. Just after midnight, the *Convert* was overtaken by some of the convoy's ships, and a few hours later gunfire erupted. Amid the confusion, the captain, John Lawford, realized he had sailed too close to some coral reefs, and in an effort to warn the rest of the convoy he hoisted his sails.

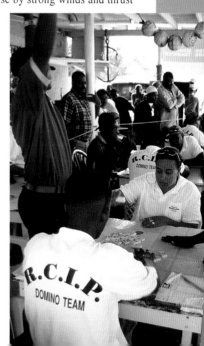

Unfortunately, the captains of the other ships took this as a sign that they were being attacked by pirates and should move closer to shore. In a matter of minutes, disaster struck. With churning seas, strong winds, and little moonlight to guide them, all 10 vessels crashed into the reef and ran aground.

Left: water-sports at the Tortuga Club
Right: serious domino players at Pirates' Cove Bar

The rough water and gusty winds prevented most of the islanders' boats from coming to the rescue. It was the daring effort of a few local fishermen who rowed out to the wrecks that saved hundreds of sailors who were flailing around in the water and clinging to the sinking ships. When it was all over, eight people were dead, but maritime historians agree that the death toll could easily have been much higher. The valiant effort of the Caymanian rescuers so impressed King George III, it is said, that he granted the Cayman Islands 'freedom from taxation in perpetuity.' Britain and America were at odds because the Americans had just declared independence, and their president, George Washington, is said to have shed no tears over the accident.

The Wreck of the Ten Sails became one of the most talked-about events in Cayman Islands' history, and inspired several books and legends. Some of the tales were false, including one claiming that Prince William, the future William IV, was on board one of the vessels. These days, the waters around Gun Bay are among the most visited dive sites in Grand Cayman. Many people come here from all over the world to catch a glimpse of the eerie relics of the ships, eight of which remain, sitting like ghosts under the sea.

Past the Memorial to the Wreck of the Ten Sails, the highway curves round the corner of the island past Sand Bluff and on to Colliers Bay.

7. SUBMARINE TOUR *(see pullout map)*

A choice of underwater tours that are particularly recommended for those who do not like diving or scuba-diving.

A submarine tour is a great alternative to diving as it allows non-divers to see the delights of the underwater world safely and comfortably without ever getting their faces wet. Several operators offer the trips, and they are all located in George Town. Most of the following day-time submarine tours depart on the hour all day long. Evening tours are scheduled three nights

a week. Advance reservations for all the tours are suggested, especially during the busy winter months.

First on the list is **Atlantis Adventures** (tel: 949 7700; approximately US$84, children under 12 US$42). This company offers more than 10 tours a day, with departures starting out from near the cruise-ship dock in George Town harbor. Atlantis use 48-passenger submarines that are spacious, air-conditioned, and surprisingly comfortable. Passengers are ferried out to the submarine in an open-top boat and then climb one-by-one down the hatch via a narrow ladder. Inside, the cabin has a long row of seats situated down the middle, each one facing outward, and the atmosphere feels very similar to that in the interior of an airplane.

Left: a tour guide provides information on board an Atlantis submarine

Once the doors are sealed, the submarine slowly drops 100ft (30m) down the face of the Cayman wall to the ocean floor, while a tour guide explains what can be seen outside. The only other sounds to be heard are the 'oohs' and 'ahhs' of the passengers, and the gentle hum of the engines as the pilot navigates the ship. Sitting single file, passengers have their own portholes that afford amazing sights – intricate corals, sponge gardens, exotic marine creatures, and tropical fish within inches of the thick glass windows. Occasionally, scuba divers swim by the submarine and feed fish or wave. The air pressure inside the cabin feels totally natural, and the experience is not at all claustrophobic. Laminated information cards detailing the types of fish in the water hang beside each porthole and make for useful reference.

Although most of the tours only visit the reef off the harbor, others venture farther out to take a look at sunken ships. Atlantis also offers night tours when the submarine's lights guide the craft along and reveal an entirely different world that only comes to life after dark.

For a peek at the sea without being in a fully submerged vessel, both the **Nautilus Undersea Tour** (tel: 945 1355) and the **Seaworld Explorer Semi-Submarine Tour** (tel: 949 7700) offer one-hour day-time trips in ships with glass hulls that enable passengers to sit 6ft (2m) below the water's surface in a glass observatory. Located at George Town harbor, these two tours are especially good for small children, who might be frightened by the real submarine trip, and for those who worry about getting claustrophobic. While they don't have such interesting views as the deeper submarine tours, they do provide a taste of what lies below the surface.

Down to the Depths

The most detailed, fascinating, and adventurous of the Grand Cayman submarine trips is the **Deep Explorer Tour** (tel: 949 7700; approximately US$450 depending on the time of year). An authentic research vessel used by the National Geographic Society and other scientific organizations, this submarine is available for passenger use only in the Cayman Islands.

The two-passenger vessel is roughly the size of a helicopter with two seats in the forward section; the pilot sits directly behind the passengers. Compressed air tanks, ballast, and high-powered batteries hang from the bottom of the craft. The procedure is similar to that on the other submarine trips – passengers are ferried out to the submarine and then climb inside. This one, however, is much, much smaller, much more confining, and not air-conditioned, so it's definitely not for those who suffer from claustrophobia.

Above: visitors try out a submarine while still on dry land

grand cayman

Gently, it drops down to about 1,000ft (305m) below the surface. Unlike the larger submarines that constantly move backward and forward, the *Deep Explorer* does not undertake much horizontal movement and most of the trip is purely vertical.

What passengers get to see is a layer-cake of marine life that changes drastically as the vessel descends deeper, and encompasses several different marine zones that range from light, bright coral reefs, to a spooky moonscape terrain when you get closer to the edge of the Cayman Trench. Down at 1,000ft (305m), there really isn't much marine life to see except for bizarre-looking fish with very large eyes, and six-gill sharks that live only in the deep, but the experience of having gone down to such depths (something few people have ever done) is what the appeal of this trip is all about.

Cozy Option

While it only goes down to about 40ft (12m), a more cozy tour option is a ride on the *Seamobile* with **Cayman Submarines** (tel: 916 3483; approximately US$169). These small submarines, which are under water for about 40 minutes, take only two passengers at a time, and have pilots wearing dive gear who ride on the outside of the vessel and navigate from behind and outside the passenger compartment while giving a narrated tour at the same time. Featuring personalized tours with an unobstructed view from the cabin, Cayman Submarines will take passengers wherever they wish to go – down the face of the Cayman Wall, to specific dive sites, or to sunken ships. They will also chase after sharks, stingrays, or turtles if you ask them to.

For all the submarine trips – day or night, shallow or deep – passengers should note that a camera flash is useless because it reflects off the glass portholes, and only film with an ASA rating of 1,000 is capable of capturing the images of the deep.

Above: descending a narrow ladder into the submarine's interior

8. THE BOTANIC PARK AND MASTIC TRAIL *(see map, p48)*

Spend a morning exploring the lush tropical gardens of Queen Elizabeth II Botanic Park with an option to hike through the Mastic Trail.

While few people pack hiking boots when they go to Grand Cayman, they do come in handy for a trek through the wilder regions of the island. It's a good idea to make this trip in the morning before the sun gets too strong. Even then, be sure to lather on the sunblock, wear a hat, and spray yourself liberally with mosquito repellent. For a thorough look round, plan on scheduling a few hours for the visit.

Located in the deep interior of the island, **Queen Elizabeth II Botanic Park** (daily 9am–6.30pm; admission fee; tel: 947 9462) is a 65-acre (26-ha) nature preserve that offers visitors a glimpse of what the island was like before tourism came to town. Several tour operators offer trips to the park, or you can make the 45-minute drive from George Town by taking Red Bay Road and continuing east along the coast until you get to Frank Sound.

Here, turn left onto Frank Sound Road and a few miles along a sign points to a wide, paved road lined with towering palms and the park entrance.

This is the Cayman Islands' premier show garden, a masterpiece of nature that came to life in 1991 after hundreds of volunteers (including schoolchildren and prisoners) spent thousands of hours clearing the land, surveying the area, and identifying and documenting trees and plants. In 1993 it won *Islands* magazine's Ecotourism Award for the finest ecotourism project in the Caribbean. Although it had been in existence for a few years, the park was 'officially' opened by Queen Elizabeth II in 1994, during her second visit to the Cayman Islands. More recently, a modern, two-story **Visitors'**

Centre was added. Equipped with a well-stocked café and gift shop, it offers plenty of information about the park. It also has interpretive exhibits that explain the flora and fauna of the islands, and occasionally hosts lectures and demonstrations. An informative exhibit in the park describes the island's many poisonous plants, such as maiden plum, which has a sap similar to poison ivy, and machineel, a plant with an extremely toxic and irritating sap.

According to Park Director, Andrew Guthrie, about 50 percent of Grand Cayman's 678 species of indigenous plants are found growing naturally in the park, and there is also a host of bird and animal life. The preserve also contains several species of rare plants found nowhere else in the world. The clearly marked **Woodland Trail** guides hikers through about 1 mile (2km) of dense woodland with a series of panels offering information about the plants. The natu-

Above: exotic flora in the Queen Elizabeth II Botanic Park
Right: a lot of watering is necessary to keep the vegetation in good shape

ral habitats change about every 100 yards (91m), depending on the type of soil and the elevation, and include wetlands, cactus thickets, logwood swamps, air-plant woodlands, thatch-palm hammocks, and mahogany forests. Not far from the trail, wild orchids and bromeliads thrive in a small pool fed by a buttonwood swamp.

Inside the park is a 2-acre (0.8-ha), man-made lake whose lily-pond areas are home to many native aquatic birds, including a large flock of whistling ducks, herons, stilts, coots, teals, and egrets. Originally part of the adjacent swamp, the brackish water lake is only about 3ft (1m) deep, but has three small islands in the center, with native vegetation.

Flowers, Heritage, and Iguanas

Overlooking the lake is the outrageously beautiful **Floral Colour Garden**, a 2.5-acre (1-ha) patch of land with hundreds of varieties of exotic, flowering plants, native and foreign, that bloom year-round. Arranged according to color, the flower patches slide through the rainbow from pink to red to orange, then yellow to blue and purple. Many of these plants are used for research as well as being part of a cooperative propagation program for botanists in other parts of the Caribbean. Nearby is a cascading waterfall that flows from a freshwater pond where dozens of turtles live, and a little tea-house that serves refreshments.

Perhaps the most interesting aspect of the park is the 2-acre (0.8-ha) **Heritage Garden**. The centerpiece is a perfectly restored wooden cottage, brought here from East End in 1995. An excellent example of classic Caymanian architecture, the pastel-painted cottage is furnished with antiques and includes a wide front porch, a cook room, a cistern, and a well, all reminiscent of life on the island 100 years ago.

Originally, the three-room structure was home to a Caymanian family with nine children. Along with a traditional sand yard, it has a small garden full of plants commonly found in early gardens, such as crotons, lilies, cat claws, tea bushes, and medicinal plants and herbs such as aloe vera.

There is an abundance of Cayman blue iguanas wandering around the garden. As part of an island-wide effort by the National Trust to protect the endemic Cayman blue, the park has implemented a breeding program that collects the iguanas from other parts of the islands then releases them here. About 30 of them have been placed in a breeding pen on the property, that is also used to conduct scientific research. In addi-

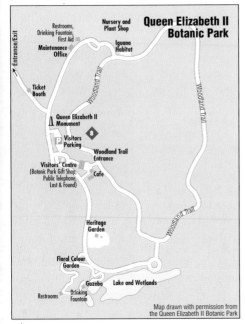

Map drawn with permission from the Queen Elizabeth II Botanic Park tion to the iguanas, there are tree frogs, lizards, and harmless snakes.

The Mastic Trail

If a hike through the Botanic Park does not satisfy your appetite for nature, you could visit the **Mastic Trail**. Located on the west side of Frank Sound Road, a few miles from the Botanic Park, the trail is not easily accessible and it is usually necessary to hire a local guide. Thirty percent of the trail remains closed due to hurricane damage. The office of the National Trust for the Cayman Islands in George Town (tel: 949 0045) arranges escorted morning and afternoon tours, as does a company called **Silver Thatch Excursions** (tel: 945 6588). Both provide transportation to and from the trail, as well as cold drinks along the way. Silver Thatch is owned by Geddes Hislop, a Caymanian-born biologist trained in Canada, who was involved in the formation of the Queen Elizabeth II Botanic Park. His tours are highly regarded by nature lovers and are considered the best in the Cayman Islands.

First created over 200 years ago, when residents of the North Shore area used it as a source of timber for export and building materials, and used thereafter as the route for herding cattle across the island, the Mastic Trail traverses one of the last tracts of primary evergreen woodland left on Grand Cayman. It gets its name from the giant mastic trees that grow naturally on the land. Before roads were built in the area, the Mastic Trail was used for many years as a thoroughfare, and after the roads were built it became overgrown. In 1994 the National Trust for the Cayman Islands adopted it as a pet restoration project. The Trust cleared the path, and a year later reopened it as an attraction for visitors interested in the island's vegetation and its past.

A traditional footpath that cuts through from the interior to the island's north shore, it winds for several miles through ancient, dry woodlands, mangrove swamps, rock formations, and farming areas. It also contains what is jokingly referred to as 'the mountain,' a rise of dirt which, at 60ft (18m) above sea level is the highest point in Grand Cayman. Dense and rugged and teeming with birds, it contains over 100 species of trees and more than 500 species of plants, and has a distinctly primeval atmosphere that enables you to imagine what the island looked like 1,000 years ago. Wild banana orchids are often in full bloom, and because it is so thick with plant life, it feels like a tunnel with only brief rays of sunlight passing through.

Above: a vivid hibiscus bloom
Right: exploring the Woodland Trail

grand cayman

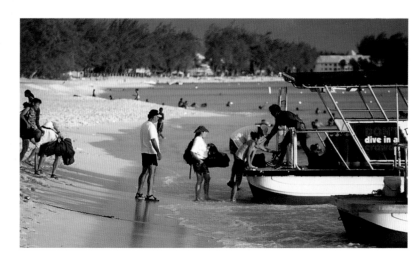

9. DIVING IN GRAND CAYMAN *(see pullout map)*

A round-up of choices for exploring the best dive spots around Grand Cayman, including Orange Canyon, Trinity Caves, the Cali Wreck, Bat's Cave, and the Wreck of the Ten Sails.

Since the 1950s, Grand Cayman has been a large gold star on the map of the world's greatest scuba destinations, and advanced divers often describe the underwater experience here as addictive. Dramatic wall diving (around a reef wall or drop off), phenomenal visibility, womb-like water temperatures, breathtaking marine life, historic shipwrecks, and a dive industry with a long reputation for responsibility – Grand Cayman has it all.

The exhilarating underwater atmosphere has raised the awareness of the islands' role as a scuba destination. World-renowned scuba diver Jean-Michel Cousteau (son of Jacques) is the official spokesperson for Cayman Islands' scuba diving and snorkeling. 'I look forward to helping the Cayman Islands continue their tradition of marine protection and to be a model for other destinations around the world,' said Cousteau. He also plays a large part in the local decision-making process regarding environmental protection, sustainable tourism, and responsible water sports.

To appreciate how amazing the diving is you should try it. But you can't just strap on a tank and dive in. Recreational diving is regulated worldwide by several independent organizations including PADI, NAUI, and SSI, and you must have proof that you've passed at least a basic dive course before any operator will take you aboard. Fortunately for novices, dozens of programs are available throughout Grand Cayman and the other islands that offer a variety of scuba lessons, ranging from one-day scuba resort courses to master level four-day certification classes. However, you can start diving sooner if you are certified before you arrive.

Be aware that strict marine park laws are enforced in the Cayman Islands, and all divers are expected to utilize dive flags or markers, must never remove anything from the water, and must not go deeper than 100ft (30m).

Above: setting off for a dive excursion

Although scuba diving is the best way to really experience the thrill of being underwater in the Cayman Islands, there are also many places where the snorkeling is divine. Most scuba guidebooks list hundreds of designated dive sites around Grand Cayman, so the list of choices can be overwhelming. A few of the sites, however, are considered unmissable by many experienced divers, and the following is a round-up of some of those favorite spots to which people return time after time.

West Coast, George Town, and Southern Sites

Starting off on the west side of the island, which is protected from the trade winds, the area near West Bay is like a salt-water swimming pool. One of the most vivid sites here is **Orange Canyon**. With visibility exceeding 100ft (30m), this deep site fairly close to the beach is a spectacular kaleidoscope of bright orange, elephant-ear sponges, coral pinnacles, and a narrow cave. Nearby is **Trinity Caves**, a coral mass that slopes down the edge of the wall through a series of chimneys, arches, and gullies. Three main canyons alternate, with ridges dropping from about 50ft (15m) on the top of the reef

to almost 100ft (30m), and are marked by black corals, deep-water sea fans, lobster, shrimp, and a variety of fish.

About 50yds (45m) away from Trinity Caves is **Cemetery Wall Reef**. Located off a waterfront cemetery, this patch reef lies in less than 10ft (3m) of water very close to shore and is marked by elkhorn corals and hundreds of fish that like to be fed by hand.

A bit to the south near Seven Mile Beach is **Paradise Reef**, a shallow dive with little or no current. Here, lots of sea fans, sea plumes, and friendly fish are the main draw. Adjacent to Paradise is the *Oro Verde* **Wreck**, the first man-made dive site ever created in Grand Cayman. This 181-ft (55-m) ship was intentionally sunk here in 1980 – before that, it is said to have been used by drug smugglers. Now it lies on its port side with the bow facing north. Although broken up quite a bit by winter storms, it is covered with marine life, including garden eels, grouper, snapper, and crabs.

Offshore from George Town are the *Cali* **Wreck** and the *Balboa*. The Cali is a shallow dive with a maximum depth of 20ft (6m). Sunk here in 1944, the *Cali* was a 220-ft (67-m) four-masted schooner that was blown up by the British Corps of Army Engineers in 1957. It is now scattered in pieces on the ocean floor, but its winches, boilers, and hull plates are all recognizable. Since it is very close to the surface, many snorkelers, as well as scuba divers, visit

Above: a diver at the reef off George Town
Right: fire coral wafting in the water

this site. A bit farther out than the *Cali* is the *Balboa,* a 375-ft (114-m) lumber steamer that was wrecked off George Town during a hurricane in 1932. Like the *Cali,* it was blown up because it was a navigation hazard, and is now strewn over a wide area. Both the *Cali* and the *Balboa* are filled with marine life, and are often used as night dive sites.

Not far away is the **Wreck of the *Gamma***, an old freighter that has been sitting on the ocean floor here for decades. The ship's rusty, orange-colored hull is half exposed and half submerged and presents a striking view. Shore access is easy from a coral cove, and the submerged part of the ship serves as home to many varieties of fish.

Also near George Town is **Devil's Grotto**, a shallow dive marked by a single-pin mooring buoy on the south side of the reef. A very popular spot, the Grotto is full of gullies and crevices with lots of tarpon swimming around. Nearby is **Parrot's Reef**, another shallow dive, directly offshore from South Church Street. An excellent spot for underwater photography, it is often used as a training dive site and, along with coral heads, includes the remains of a small tugboat used as an *Atlantis* submarine tender, which sank during a storm in 1987. A little bit south of Parrot's Reef is **Waldo's Reef**. Named in honor of its most famous resident, a moray eel known as Waldo, this shallow site is filled with numerous tame fish and a bunch of barracuda.

Moving along the south side of the island we come to **Oriental Gardens** and **Japanese Gardens**, both just offshore on the outskirts of George Town. Shallow dives marked by a single-pin mooring buoy, they are lovely sites with acres of brightly-colored staghorn coral, sea plumes, soft corals, and schooling fish.

Also in this area is **Dangerous Dan Drop-Off**, a deep and dramatic dive. A large coral buttress cut with ravines and under-hanging coral gardens, Dangerous Dan's is swarming with marine life, including lots of spotfin hogfish. Not far away is **Bat's Cave**, an intricate and extensive tunnel and cave system with a profusion of elkhorn coral and lots of lobsters and shrimp.

East End and the North

Off the East End of Grand Cayman is the most famous site in all the Cayman Islands, the **Wreck of the Ten Sails** *(see page 43)*. Here, the somber remains of 10 British merchant ships that sank in 1794 attract divers from around the world and offer a haunting glimpse of Caymanian maritime history. Although not as dramatic, another popular site fairly close to the Ten Sails is **The Maze**. A deep dive that often has choppy currents, The Maze features a honeycomb of tunnels with several swim-throughs that meander into

Left: a Caribbean reef shark swims through the deep blue waters dark caves and fissures and then out again into light blue seas. Two resident bull sharks are a common sight, as are black coral fans, deep-water gorgonian fans, and dense formations of brain coral.

A few miles north east of The Maze is **Shark Alley**, a deep dive prone to rip tides from the channel. Although it is considered very difficult, Shark Alley can make for an exciting dive, due to the many large boulders, coral buttresses, small caves, and pristine sponges. Also in the East End is *Ridgefield* **Reef**, a shallow site prone to currents. The *Ridgefield* was a 441-ft (144-m) Liberian freighter weighing over 7,000 tons/tonnes that ran aground here in 1962. Today, it is almost entirely coated with algae, corals, sea fans, and marine life. The last place of note in this part of the island is **Snapper Hole**, one of the top dive sites in Grand Cayman. A shallow dive with good visibility, Snapper Hole has an amazing mass of large caves and fissures inside the reef's structure. It's a fascinating spot, full of coral growth, schools of tarpon, tunnels lined with eels and lobsters, and has a rusty old anchor embedded in the top of the reef.

Along the northern coast of Grand Cayman, the underwater atmosphere is world famous for its sheer drop-off points with higher than average visibility. A few of the more popular sites include **Haunted House**, a deep dive to the east of Rum Point Channel. What looks like a large amphitheater is formed out of two coral buttresses and is covered in coral trees, black barrel sponges, turtles, and rays. **No Name Wall**, a deep dive with moderate currents, is noted for a series of four perpendicular ravines that plunge over the wall. Not far from No Name is **Chinese Wall**, a canyon with a cave-like opening that has three large buttress formations, and a profusion of black coral, sponges, trumpet fish, grouper, snapper, and tiny shrimp. In the east, close to Old Man Bay is **Babylon**, a series of ravines with brilliant rope sponges, pristine corals, and large schools of fish. Heading west toward Morgans Harbor, you come to **Ghost Mountain**, a deep dive for intermediate to advanced divers. Noted for its large coral pinnacle lying in a sand slope at about 140ft (43m), Ghost Mountain is almost always full of large schools of fish.

Above: stop-light parrot fish swim among bluehead wrasse coral

Cayman Brac

One of the two 'little sisters' of the Cayman Islands, Cayman Brac is 89 miles (143km) northeast of Grand Cayman. Twelve miles (19km) long by 1 mile (1.6km) wide, it has a resident population of about 1,600 and topographically is the most interesting of the islands. Brac is the Gaelic word for bluff, and the island's rugged limestone bluff that dominates the interior rises to 140ft (43m), marked by honey-combed caves and a fascinating array of vegetation.

Far less developed than Grand Cayman, Cayman Brac is made up of a friendly, close-knit community of people known as Brackers, most of whom are descendants of Caymanian seafarers. It also has a small but solid ex-pat community of people who have fallen in love with the peace and quiet of the island, and the quality of life it affords them.

Until the mid-1960s there were only 10 phone lines on the island, and electricity didn't appear until 1966. Although there has been a modest amount of development in the past 10 years, Cayman Brac is still a place where people rarely lock their doors, and motorists wave to each other as they pass. Although it is small in size, it has every amenity a visitor could want, including good hotels, restaurants, and plenty of fun things to explore. There's even a small hospital, in case of emergency.

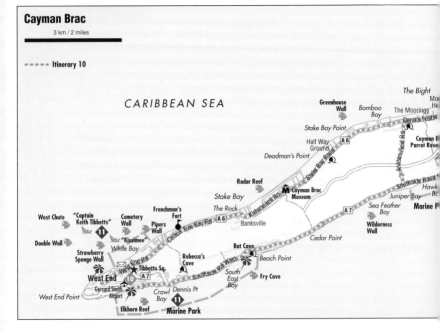

Cayman Brac

3 km / 2 miles

- - - - - **Itinerary 10**

Departing from the George Town airport, both Cayman Airways and Island Air *(see Practical Information, page 81 for details)* provide a 40-minute flight to Cayman Brac. The entire island can be seen in one day, but an overnight trip is suggested, especially if you want to do some diving, and renting a car for the day will enable you to explore the lesser known nooks and crannies of the island at your leisure.

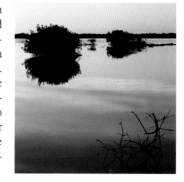

10. HIGHLIGHTS OF CAYMAN BRAC *(see map below)*

An overnight trip to Cayman Brac with a hike along the bluff, and visits to the Bat Cave, NIM's Cottage, and the Cayman Brac Museum.

As soon as you land at the small **Gerard Smith Airport**, you realize you have left the intensity of Grand Cayman far behind. Tourists introduce themselves to each other, offer tips about diving in the area, and act as if they are part of a family reunion. Even the car rental agencies are casual. Upon departure many simply ask that you leave the car at the airport with keys in the ash tray.

Most of the major hotels are within minutes of the airport on the western end of the island, and after checking in, you can start your day tour. This area is also where the best beaches are and the swimming is terrific. Driving east on the one road along the coast, this stretch is called Southside Road West, you will spot, on the left, the **Westerly Ponds**, two salt-water bodies of water dotted with mangrove islands. Oblivious to the airport noise, the ponds are bird sanctuaries, home to hundreds of ducks, egrets, stilts, and herons. An occasional white barn owl may be spotted, perched high in a tree. A short way past the Westerly Ponds is the **Salt Water Pond**, another marshy bird rookery, and past this a small sign points toward a gravel road leading to **Rebecca's Cave**. This large opening in the limestone bluff is the grave-site of Rebecca Bodden, a baby who died during the 1932 hurricane.

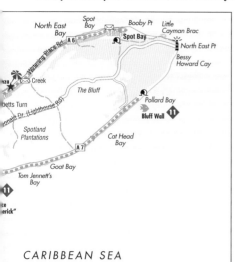

CARIBBEAN SEA

Left: local garage owner
Above: a salt-water pond

Nearby is **Bat Cave**, a large cave that has been used for over 100 years as a shelter during hurricanes. Along with most of the other caves on Cayman Brac, this one is maintained by the National Trust, and is kept in excellent condition, with guide rails and ladders to assist hikers who want to explore it. A two-level cave with wooden steps and an enormous opening, Bat Cave is very accessible and offers a panoramic view of the sea.

Continuing on for several miles, the road passes a few hotels and many private homes built right on the coast, and eventually comes to a dead end

at **Pollard Bay**. To the left, the towering bluff gradually gets higher the farther east you travel along the road. At just about any point along here you can park on the shoulder and climb up the bluff to take a short hike. There are several footpaths and trails that traverse the bluff and wind past cacti, wild orchids, and thatch palms. The green parrot is commonly seen here, as are soldier crabs and lizards.

About mid-point along this road is **Ashton Reid Road**, the island's intersection. Turn left and in about ½ mile (1km) you will spot a gravel road that runs through the center of the island. Deep in the interior, not far from here, is the **Cayman Brac Parrot Reserve**, a 180-acre (73-ha) parcel of land designed to protect indigenous plants as well as the Cayman Brac parrot. Continue for another ½ mile (1km) and you'll see goats and cattle in adjoining fields, and wild native plum and West Indian cherry trees growing, before you emerge on the North Shore of Cayman Brac.

NIM's Things

Turning right here will take you along the coast past fishing boats and small homes painted bright Caribbean colors with tin roofs and small vegetable gardens out front. Less than 1 mile (1.5km) up the road is **La Esperanza** (tel: 948 0531), a wonderful waterfront eatery featuring authentic Caymanian cuisine; their weekly barbecues are legendary. Farther along you will come to **Spot Bay** and eventually see **NIM's** (Mon–Sat 9am–6pm; tel: 948 0461), a small cottage shop and home to Tenson Scott. A native Caymanian, Scott is one of the few people on the island who is allowed to remove the caymanite stone from the bluff, and his hand-made jewelry is known throughout the islands. With pick and maul, he carefully chips away the stone, and then laboriously turns it into brownish-orange masterpieces. Now in his seventies, Scott is a friendly man who can tell wonderful tales of life on Cayman Brac – and he's an experienced fisherman who can point you toward the best spots to drop a line. His shop, whose initials stand for Native Island Made, is full of his jewelry, straw hats, and local arts and crafts. Beyond NIM's the road ends at the eastern edge of the island where the rugged coastline, marked by crashing waves, is often dotted with driftwood and nautical debris.

Above: Bat Cave has always been used as a hurricane shelter, and is very accessible for those who want to explore its secrets.

Stake Bay

Backtracking down the coast, past the turn-off point to Ashton Reid Road, is an area of Cayman Brac known as Stake Bay, a small community that is home to the **Government Administration Building**, a duty-free store, and the small **Faith Hospital**. A few steps away from the government offices is the **Cayman Brac Museum** (Mon–Fri 9am–noon, 1–4pm, Sat 9am–noon; free; tel: 948 2622). A white clapboard building with swing seats on the front porch, it once housed the island's post office, customs bureau, treasury, and bank, and still contains the booths of those offices.

Transformed into a museum in 1983, it now houses a large and impressive collection of artifacts and antiques that explain the island's history and offer a taste of what life was like for the early Irish, Scottish, and English settlers. Housed in glass cases, its treasures include old photographs, anchors, turtle shells, crocodile hides, hurricane lamps, wooden radios, hand-written news bulletins, carpenters' tools, sewing machines, clothing, and butter churns. It also tells the story of the brutal 1932 hurricane that killed 109 people. It just about wiped out the entire island, and still lingers in the minds of many Brackers. William Ryan, the museum's curator, is always on hand to answer questions and explain the significance of the items on display.

Leaving the museum, take the coastal road that continues to the western end of the island, toward the airport, passes a few cafés and several churches, and eventually runs into **Tibbetts Square**. A modern, strip-mall shopping center, Tibbetts Square is the island's main commercial center, where most local people come for their supplies. It includes a large, well-stocked grocery store and a cute little boutique called the **Treasure Chest**. Owned by Hyacynth Scott, a native Caymanian with family roots dating back over 100 years, the Treasure Chest sells tropical clothing, jewelry, hats, and souvenirs. Next door is **Ed's Place**, a casual watering hole where local people come to share the latest gossip.

Top: enjoy a Caymanian lunch at La Esperanza.
Right a model boat at the Cayman Brac Museum

11: Diving in Cayman Brac *(see map, p54–5)*

This itinerary offers a few hours diving in Cayman Brac. There are several sites to choose from, including the *Tibbetts* Wreck, Strawberry Sponge Wall, the *Kissimee* Wreck, Fry Cave, and the *Prince Frederick* Wreck.

Many of the resorts on Cayman Brac have full-service dive operators on site with certified scuba masters on staff, and are equipped with dive boats, gear, air, and anything else a visiting scuba diver might need. Most lead regularly-scheduled trips to various locations several times a day, and there is a weekly night dive. You can also shore dive by day and night with buddies.

Although the dive sites off Cayman Brac are very similar to those on Grand Cayman, there are far fewer divers in the waters here. This means the coral reefs are less disturbed and therefore in better shape. It also means, in the minds of many divers, that Cayman Brac is a far more prestigious and exclusive location than Grand Cayman. There are about 50 documented dive sites scattered around the little island, and the following are just a few of the most popular.

One of the most visited and most dramatic sites is ***Tibbetts* Wreck**. A Russian destroyer intentionally sunk here in 1996 by Jean-Michel Cousteau, the MV *Captain Keith Tibbetts* is now a flagship of marine conservation. Amid a great deal of fanfare as the destroyer was sinking, Cousteau stood on the deck in full scuba gear, holding on to the guard rails as the ship gradually vanished from sight.

Over 300ft (92m) long and 42ft (13m) wide, the destroyer was part of an old Soviet fleet stationed in Cuba during the Cold War years. It was acquired by the Cayman government after the break-up of the Soviet Union, with the goal of creating an artificial reef to aid marine life in these waters. These days, it is covered in algae and other marine growth and makes for a

Above: rock beauty coral, an underwater delight

captivating dive in about 75ft (23m) of water off the west end of the island. Barracudas, groupers and angel fish are a familiar sight around the wreck.

Not far from Tibbetts Wreck is **Double Wall**, a deep dive with a steeply fissured reef crust and small ledge. Along with the remains of a private wreck, Double Wall has lots of fish and a profusion of sponges.

Continuing along the north coast of the west end of the island you reach **West Chute**, another deep dive, this one with very steep sand chutes, huge barrel sponges, and lots of hermit crabs and squirrel fish.

Next comes **Strawberry Sponge Wall**. As the name implies, this 75-ft (23-m) site has a lovely reef wall cut by overhangs that are adorned with beautiful strawberry vase sponges. It also has lots of starfish and thousands of garden eels.

The *Kissimee* **Wreck**, to the northeast of Strawberry Sponge Wall, is a shallow dive marked by a single-pin mooring. In 1982, this retired tugboat, now sitting on her port side, was deliberately sunk to supplement the natural reef system, and is now a great favorite with photographers.

Not far away, to the east, is **Cemetery Wall**. A deep dive with deep fissures, this site is marked by large star coral, black coral, butterfly fish, and angel fish. Nearby are **Pipers Wall** and **Charlie's Reef**. Piper's has enormous canyons with pretty sea fans and black coral as well as long tube sponges. Charlie's is a shallow spot noted for its large elkhorn and staghorn corals.

South Coast Sites

Over on the opposite – south – coast is **Elkhorn Reef**, a shallow dive with four deep ridges and many gullies, canyons, and swim-throughs. It also has a huge brain coral that is almost always swarming with barracuda. **Fry Cave**, a shallow site with moderate currents, also has lots of canyons and gullies as well as plenty of arrow crabs, yellow stingrays, pistol shrimp, and crabs. Sometimes called Cio's Craig, **Wilderness Wall** is a deep dive with a moderate current. With a good reef crest and wide sandy plateau, Wilderness has some excellent coral formations, lots of chimneys cutting through the vertical wall, and coral canyons and arches.

Continuing along in an northeasterly direction, you next come to the *Prince Frederick* **Wreck**, a twin-masted, wooden-hulled schooner said to have sunk here in the latter part of the 19th century. About 100ft (30m) long, the wreck includes an anchor, chains, scrap metal, and lots of copper nails.

The last on the list is **Bluff Wall**, an extremely dramatic site with steep vertical drops and deep fissures, large sea fans, black coral, pink sponges, sharks, turtles, hermit crabs, and stingrays. Whichever site you choose, you are guaranteed a diving experience that will linger in your memory long after your vacation is over.

Right: a queen angel fish, one of many species that can be seen beneath the waters of Cayman Brac

Little Cayman

The baby of the Cayman Islands trio, Little Cayman is indeed little. Located 74 miles (120km) northeast of Grand Cayman, and just 7 miles (11km) from Cayman Brac, it is 10 miles (16km) long by 1 mile (1.6km) wide. A small, safe, tropical haven, Little Cayman has a resident population of about 150 people, most of whom know each other by first name. It also has one grocery store, one bank (open only on Wednesday), one small cemetery, and one school teacher, who flies in each day from Cayman Brac to preside over the education of about five local children.

In the late 1980s the island had a population of 12; there were three phone lines and no electricity. Although dozens of houses and hotels have been built since then, the National Trust has passed laws ensuring that no chain hotels or restaurants will ever come to Little Cayman. Most of the people who live here are foreigners rather than Caymanians, and they either work in the tourism industry or come to stay in their private vacation retreats.

Little Cayman's earliest visitors were pirates who used it as a base while plundering ships in nearby waters. In the early 1950s a group of American fishermen set up a camp that eventually turned into the Southern Cross Club, a popular fishing and dive resort. Today, most visitors are divers and fishermen, but the island also gets a handful of nature lovers who come to see the numerous exotic birds and more than 2,000 rock iguanas that live amid the tropical foliage. Road signs warn drivers: 'Iguanas Have the Right of Way.' All supplies on the island are either shipped in or flown in daily from George Town.

Departing from either George Town or Cayman Brac, Island Air *(see page 81, for details)* has several flights a day in small propeller planes. Although the island can be seen in a day, an overnight stay is recommended, especially if you want to dive. Many of the hotels provide transportation to sites around the island, or you can rent a car or use one of the resorts' bicycles.

12. HIGHLIGHTS OF LITTLE CAYMAN   *(see map below)*

An overnight trip to Little Cayman Island with visits to Booby Pond Nature Reserve, the National Trust House, and Little Cayman Museum.

The bumpy grass landing strip and one-room shack that serves as the **Edward Bodden Airfield** is the first impression that newcomers have of the island, and one that usually makes them smile. Two large iguanas live in the airport grounds, and often startle guests on their way to the public bathrooms behind the airport shack. After checking in to their resorts (most hotels collect guests from the airport), visitors can't wait to take a leisurely look round the circumference of the unspoiled island.

Less than 1 mile (1.6km) from the airport is **Blossom Village Square**, a tiny, strip shopping mall and so-called town center that houses the island's only

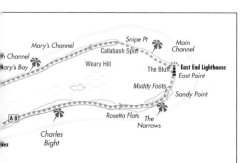

Mary's Channel
Snipe Pt
Main Channel
h Channel
Callabash Spot
ary's Bay
Weary Hill
The Bluff
East End Lighthouse
East Point
Muddy Foots
Sandy Point
A 8
Rosetta Flats
The Narrows
Charles Bight
ies

CARIBBEAN SEA

····· Itinerary 12

Little Cayman

1.6 km / 1 mile

Above: one of over 2,000 iguanas on Little Cayman

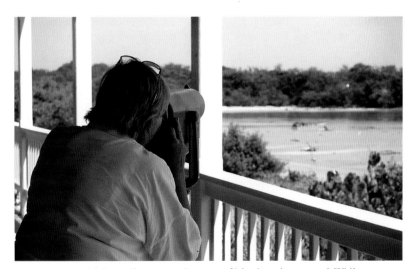

grocery/hardware/liquor store, Internet café, bank, and newsstand. While you won't find *The New York Times* here, you will find current issues of *Caymanian Compass*, flown in daily from George Town. You can also stock up on whatever supplies you forgot to bring with you. Nearby, the **Hungry Iguana** is a terrific island-style restaurant and one of the few on Little Cayman that doesn't belong to a resort.

Owen Island

As you travel farther along the road (it's the only one, and it makes a 22-mile (35-km) loop around the entire island), several dive resorts appear along the coast, and then the paved road surface turns to packed dirt and sand. Several shallow ponds, dotted with dense foliage, can be seen on the left side of the road. Offshore in the distance you can spot **Owen Island**, sometimes called Cayman's fourth island. Owen Island used to be connected to Little Cayman by a sand spit, but that has long gone. About 230 yds (210 m) east of the shore, this 11-acre (4.5-ha) private island has a beautiful, sandy beach dotted with palms and is often used by local hotels for afternoon picnic excursions. You can also swim to the island on your own.

On the left side of the road you will spot a sign that says **Booby Pond Nature Reserve**. An inland, salt-water lagoon, Booby Pond is a United Nations-designated Ramsar wetland site over 1 mile (1.6km) long (such sites are named after a convention in Ramsar, Iran). A few years ago a sprawling **National Trust House** was built here with a modern visitors' center, complete with a wooden walkway to the rear and high-powered telescopes for viewing birds. Inside the Trust House, museum-quality exhibits describe the flora and fauna of the island.

Above: bird-watching at Booby Pond
Right: visitors relax at Pirates Point Resort

At the back, the view of the rookery is spectacular. About 20,000 red-footed boobies live here and the commotion they cause at dusk is amazing. Carrying freshly-caught fish in their claws, they swoop in to find a perch for the night in the trees. There are also hundreds of frigate birds that circle above on the warm, thermal air currents and then join in the action. In the winter months the frigates puff up their chests and throats and do a little mating dance. In addition to the frigates and boobies, more than 150 species of resident and migratory birds can be seen on Little Cayman, including ducks, cranes, egrets, herons, and parrots. Other wildlife includes hermit crabs, turtles, frogs, and, of course, iguanas.

A few yards away and on the opposite side of the road from the National Trust House is the **Little Cayman Museum** (Mon, Wed, Thur, and Fri 3–5pm; free). In a tiny, white wooden building with lots of island character, the museum exhibits tell the stories of the colorful pirates who once camped out on the island, and the ship-building and seafaring traditions of the early settlers in the mid-19th century. Among the interesting artifacts on display are old family photographs, nautical antiques, island-made furniture, turtle shells, clothing, tools, thatch-rope, cooking utensils, household goods, and china tea cups that trace the lineage of the British royal family. A few steps north from the museum is the recently-built **Baptist Church of Little Cayman**.

Natural Habitats

Continuing on the road you will reach **Tarpon Lake**, a landlocked 15-acre (6-ha) stretch of water that attracts migratory birds and is brimming with tarpon fish. A small boardwalk leads visitors on a trail along parts of the lake's shore. The coastal road then continues round the eastern end of the island past the **East End Lighthouse** and an area called **Snipe Point**. It then heads down the northern coast, past private homes perched by the sea.

As you round the bend of the island, heading south back toward the airport, you will come to the **Salt Rocks Nature Trail**. This trail, through a dense woodland area, is thick with mahogany and palm trees, cactus bushes, and bromeliads, and passes the remains of an old railroad car that served a phosphate strip-mining plant, which once operated on the land. On Sunday morning, a local resident, Gladys Howard, leads walking tours along the trail. The owner of **Pirates Point Resort**, Howard is one of Little Cayman's most eccentric characters. A Texas-born gourmet chef and avid scuba diver, she has lived on Little Cayman since the 1980s, and is delightfully flamboyant and fun. If you can't catch her Sunday morning walk, stop off at her resort, have a drink at the bar, and invite her to regale you with tales of life on this small island.

Right: Tarpon Lake

13. Diving in Little Cayman *(see map, p60–61)*

A few hours' diving in the waters off Little Cayman, with a choice of spectacular sites, including the world famous Bloody Bay Wall, Paradise Plunge, Grundy's Gardens, and Soto Trader.

As on Cayman Brac, most hotels and resorts have certified scuba masters on staff and are equipped with boats, gear, air, and anything else a visiting scuba diver might need. They lead scheduled dive trips several times a day.

The waters off Little Cayman, described by the late scuba diver, Philippe Cousteau, as among the best dive sites he had ever visited, attract divers from around the world. The steep wall plunges and exquisite coral gardens around the island were what enthused Cousteau. As there is little dive traffic, the waters are almost always crystal clear. There are about 60 documented sites off Little Cayman, and a round-up of some of the more popular ones follows.

Part of the Cayman Islands Marine Park system, **Bloody Bay Wall** on the north shore is the one spot Little Cayman divers never miss. Between Jackson Point and Spot Bay, Bloody Bay has two distinct walls and over 15 recorded dive sites within it. The only wall dive in the Cayman Islands that begins its vertical leap from depths of less than 20 ft (6 m), Bloody Bay's legendary plunge has consistently clear water with visibility up to 150 ft (45 m). Local rules restrict the number of divers on each visiting boat to 20. The bay, a deep indigo abyss, is marked by winding ravines, deep crevices, coral gardens, and pristine sponges, and it is usually filled with an amazing array of marine life, including eagle rays, yellow-fin groupers, sea turtles, horse-eye jacks, parrotfish, grunts, and creole-fish.

Nearby is **Great Wall West** with a sheer and sudden drop from 18 ft (5.5 m) to more than 2,000 ft (610 m) and a bounty of yellow sea horses, lettuce-leaf plants, and reef dwellers. **Randy's Gazebo** is also near Bloody Bay Wall.

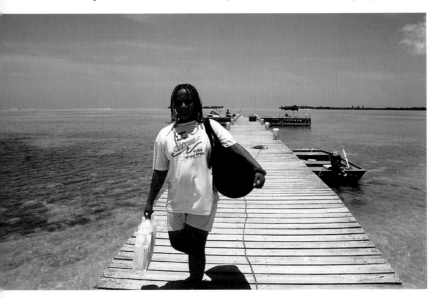

Above: coming ashore on a Little Cayman jetty

Sometimes known as The Arch, Randy's is a deep dive with good visibility and a series of deep grooves with caves and swim-throughs, and colorful marine life.

Just south of Randy's Gazebo is **Paradise Plunge**. A single-pin buoy marks this spot, with little current on the inner reef. Here, the wall plunges in a series of overhangs covered in rope sponges and pink vase sponges. Deeper down are long sea whips and small clumps of star coral.

To the northeast of Paradise Plunge is **Eagle Ray Roundup** and **Nancy's Cup of Tea**. Eagle Ray is marked by a twin-barrel mooring buoy and contains a gentle sand slope with a natural amphitheater, usually bustling with stingrays, barjacks, eagle rays, hogfish, and snapper. In the evening, especially in summer, enormous manta rays gather in this spot and swoop and roll through the water. At Nancy's Cup, a shallow dive with good visibility, divers marvel at the huge sponges and coral heads. The site was named after

Nancy Sefton, an accomplished diver who has written many articles and guides to the area. In Mary's Bay, to the north of Nancy's, is **Rock Bottom Wall**, a deep dive with a choppy surface. The coral reef wall is marked with coral pinnacle and barrel sponges.

The West Coast

Off the western tip of Little Cayman is **Sandcastle**, a deep dive with very little current. A relatively new and little-explored site, Sandcastle has lots of spur and groove formations and plenty of parrotfish. As you continue round the west coast, **Lighthouse Wall** is nearby. An exposed site, with waters that can get choppy, this is a weather-dependent dive, best done in summer. It has excellent coral formations on the reef's crest, fan corals, and lots of parrotfish. Further along is **Dynamite Drop-Off**. With a single-pin mooring buoy, Dynamite has little or no current. Large schools of snapper, grunts, and porkfish congregate here, and there is lots of finger and elkhorn coral.

Close to South Hole Sound, **Grundy's Gardens** is a deep dive with little current and excellent light for underwater photography. Named after Mike Grundy of the Cayman Islands Marine Conservation Unit, this coral buttress is usually dense with barracuda, hermit crabs, and marine worms. Next to Grundy's is **Soto Trader**, a shallow dive named after a ship that sank here in 1975 and now rests in 60 ft (18 m) of water, intact and fun to explore. Last on the list of sites, just south of Soto Trader, is **The Edge**, a deep dive with a moderate current. With good light for photography, this site is noted for its vertical wall filled with chutes and canyons and numerous species of butterfly fish.

Top: the evocatively-named stop-light parrotfish
Right: some people like to bring their own marine life with them

little cayman

Leisure Activities

SHOPPING

There are two things that sum up the shopping scene in the Cayman Islands: it is **duty-free** and there is **no sales tax**. The islands boast about being a shoppers' haven and purchasing is certainly a favorite activity for many visitors. This does not, however, always translate into bargains. Since most retail items are shipped in from other countries, and are then levied with import duties, the prices of goods can be steep. It's wise, therefore, to know the cost of high-priced items back home before plopping down the credit card. Also, prices in most stores are listed in Cayman Islands dollars, so remember to factor in the exchange rate.

The range of goods found here is wide – designer clothing, china, crystal, porcelain, perfumes, leather goods, liquor, Irish linens, jewelry, cameras, Cuban cigars, antique coins, and vintage maps. A few local products are also worth checking out. Several brands of **hot pepper sauce**, made from scotch bonnet peppers (very hot), onions, tomatoes, vinegar, and water, are always winners. The smooth, strong, locally made **Tortuga Rum**, Cayman's number-one export, is another favorite take-home item. So is **Tortuga Rum Cake**, a buttery, rich, and liquor-laden treat that enables you to get drunk and fat at the same time. Made from a century-old recipe, the cakes come in handsome tin containers that make good storage boxes when empty.

The other hot local item that many people find irresistible is **caymanite**, semi-precious dolomite stone thought to have been formed between 16 million and 25 million years ago. A beautiful stone found only in the Cayman Islands, it varies in color from beige to pink and brown, and when turned into pendants, rings, earrings, money clips, or key rings, makes a delightful memento or gift to take back home.

Although endangered and no longer farmed in the Cayman Islands, black coral, usually in the form of jewelry, is abundant in many stores. But buyers should beware; only jewelers licensed by the Caymanian government can sell it and unless your purchase comes with an official certificate it might be confiscated at Customs. Other items to be careful about are **turtle products** (shells, jewelry, oils, canned meat). Sold just about everywhere in the Cayman Islands, turtle products are not allowed into the US or several other countries.

While the largest concentration of stores is in downtown George Town, there are others in most busy tourist areas of Grand Cayman. Most stores in Cayman Brac and Little Cayman are tiny, and are usually in hotels.

Artifacts
Harbour Drive, George Town
Tel: 949 2442
Boutique specializing in antique maps, rare coins, coin jewelry, silver, enamel work, and antique scientific and marine instruments.

Bayshore Mall
South Church Street, George Town
Tel: 949 7477
Kirk Freeport's magnificent shopping mall, situated overlooking the George Town harbor, glistens as the home to the world's greatest names in watches, jewelry, crockery, and silverware. And it's all duty free.

Left: hats, baskets, and other items made of thatch palm are popular buys
Right: the famous Tortuga Rum Cake

Beyond the Horizon
Galleria Plaza, West Bay Road
Tel: 946 1498
Recently expanded, this store is a treasure trove of Indonesian-style furniture, beautifully decorated throws, rugs, lanterns, ornaments, cushions, and so much more.

Blackbeard Liquors
Crewe Road, George Town
Tel: 949 8763
In addition to being a full-service liquor store, this is the home of Blackbeard's Premium Rums, a locally produced rum that comes in 11 flavors, including coconut, mango, peach, and banana.

Cathy Church's Underwater Photo Gallery
Church Street, south of George Town
Tel: 949 7415
World-famous underwater photographer, Cathy Church, displays and sells her breathtaking shots of Cayman Islands' marine life and underwater topography.

Cayman Camera
Goring Avenue, George Town
Tel: 949 8359
A comprehensive array of regular and underwater cameras, loads of hi-tech photography equipment and all the necessary supplies, binoculars, and Cayman prints from local photographers.

China Boutique
Tel: 949 0084
Central George Town
Drawing inspiration from the Far East this shop stocks beautiful Oriental clothing and accessories.

Coach Leather Factory Store
Anchorage Centre, George Town
Tel: 949 7477
Duty-free leather goods from the factory of a well-known US brand, including good-quality purses, wallets, and briefcases.

Colombian Emeralds International
Harbour Drive, George Town
Tel: 949 8808
A variety of stunning emeralds; there is also a selection of tanzanite jewelry, made from a gemstone from Tanzania.

East End Garden and Gifts
Sea View Road, East End
Tel: 947 0737
About a half hour drive east from George Town is an Aladdin's cave of garden goodies overlooking the ocean at East End.

Esteban Gallery
Waterfront, George Town
Tel: 946 2787
A gallery displaying and selling the work of Horacio Esteban, one of the islands's few indigenous artists. Esteban sculpts caymanite, a multi-colored rock chipped from the bluff. The artist uses the semi-precious stone as an inlay in tables, for jewelry, and he also produces beautiful sculptures.

Far Away Places
Shedden Road, George Town
Tel: 949 7477
A luxurious Irish linen shop with sheets, pillow cases, bedspreads, shams (bed throws), Battenberg lace, and crocheted tablecloths.

Fort Street Market
Central George Town
Tel: 945 0760
A newsagent-cum-snack bar-cum-lunch spot, great if you are hungry and in a hurry. The delicious and refreshing Cayman lemonade is recommended, especially on a steamy day.

Grand Switzerland
Anchorage Shopping Centre, George Town
Tel: 946 2333
A fantastic assortment of Swiss watches, cultured pearls, black fresh-water pearls, tanzanite, sapphires, and emeralds.

Above: no breakfast, but plenty of jewelry at Tiffany's

Heritage Crafts and Gift Market
Harbour Drive, George Town
Tel: 945 6041
Classic Caribbean gifts such as straw hats, island music tapes and CDs, woodcarvings, shell jewelry, spices, teas, and coffee.

Jacques Scott
corner North Sound and Sheddon Road
Tel: 949 0277
Wine Cellar, Galleria Plaza
Tel: 945 5260
Jacques Scott brings you the finest wines, spirits, and beers on the island. Speak to Paul McLaughlin, the stores' knowledgeable manager, for information on wines to suit your taste and budget.

Joe Tourist Caribbean Village
Goring Avenue, George Town
Tel: 946 5638
Don't let the name turn you off. Part artists' retreat and part nature store, this unusual complex feels like an old Caymanian home with a thatched roof, sand floors, and tropical flowers. Owner Gilbert Nicoletta represents artists and craftsmen from all the islands and stocks calabash masks, thatch fans, and bags.

Kennedy Gallery
West Shore Centre, Seven Mile Beach
Tel: 949 8077
One of the finer galleries on the islands, Kennedy stocks an exclusive array of innovative Wassi art – Jamaican-made pottery utilizing terracotta clay and a thin mineral glaze. The bowls, vases, plates, mugs, cups, and pitchers are all one-of-a-kind pieces with painted or etched tropical scenes in vibrant colors.

Little Darlings
Alexandra Place, George Town
Tel: 949 2580
Children's clothing in all sizes and price ranges, plus toys, dolls' houses, books, and art supplies.

Oriental Market
Tel: 949 1109
Central George Town
An absolute find for lovers of Chinese cuisine, the Oriental Market is crammed full of authentic spices, sauces, curries and flavorings, as well as crockery and knick-knacks.

Pure Art
South Church Street, George Town
Tel: 949 9133
This small but clever gallery housed in an old cottage is a treasure chest of goods from more than 200 local artists. Each room is packed with colorful arts and crafts, oil paintings, watercolors, hand-carved tableware, and whimsical thatch brooms made by Caymanian artist, Conrad Forbes.

Tropical L'Attitude
Edward Street, George Town
Tel: 945 1233
A dazzling boutique filled with handcrafted gifts, hand-carved curio cabinets, batik bedspreads, hand-woven bags and baskets, and tropical-print beach wraps and sexy sarongs.

Tortuga Duty Free Liquors and Bakery
West Bay, near the Cayman Turtle Farm
Tel: 949 9247
A heady, sweet-smelling store, which is also a working bakery with a delicious assortment of rum cakes and other baked goods, bottled rums, rum creams, rum liqueurs, and souvenirs.

Venture Gallery
West Shore Centre, Seven Mile Beach
Tel: 949 8657
Maritime artifacts from centuries of Cayman Islands' history, including gold coins, nautical antiques, silver, and maps.

Waterford & Wedgewood Gallery
Cardinal Avenue, George Town
Tel: 949 7477
An exquisite collection of Waterford crystal, including champagne flutes and wine glasses, and Wedgewood china plates, cups, and decorative plaques.

Ye Olde Exotic Tattoos and Piercing
Tel: 946 5899
Aqua Mall, George Town Harbor Front
A good place to go if you are brave enough to go the whole hog and change your body forever with a tattoo or piercing.

EATING OUT

Although spiked with a sassy West Indian attitude, Cayman Islands cuisine borrows from the heritage of all the ethnic groups that have settled on the islands during the past three centuries. Starting out with the earliest settlers, from the British Isles, the islands forged a tradition of European cooking styles with an emphasis on stews, Cornish pasties, fried or cured fish, meats, and breads. The enslaved Africans brought their cultivation skills and the seeds of their homelands and added an interesting accent on vegetables and pulses. The Cayman tradition of 'jerking' meats and poultry (smoking them over burning pimento branches and wood) came from nearby Jamaica, as did the use of curry powder and Asian spices, brought to Jamaica by workers from the East Indies and China. A hint of Spanish and Portuguese spices and cooking styles also crept in, brought by mariners and settlers on Spanish-controlled islands.

As its foundation, Caymanian cuisine has always incorporated the bounty of fish, turtles, crabs, conch, and lobsters that are easily found offshore. Herbs and spices often used in Caymanian cooking include garlic, thyme, nutmeg, allspice, and pimento. Local cakes and breads, usually heavy and dense, are commonly made from cassava, yam, corn, breadfruit, or sweet potato, and usually have a splash of coconut milk added.

Typical dishes that should be tried include conch, marinated in lime and served as a spicy stew, or fried as fritters; turtle, prepared as a steak, or in a stew or soup; fish rundown, which means simmered in coconut milk with breadfruit or cassava; fish tea – a light clear soup, which some say is an aphrodisiac; Johnny cakes – dense, fried breads; pumpkin soup; meat patties; fried plantains (bananas); coconut shrimp; red bean soup; rice and peas (not peas, in fact, but red kidney beans); jerk chicken or beef; sautéed *callaloo* (spinach-like greens); and freshly squeezed papaya, mango, and guava juice.

There are over 300 restaurants on these three small islands (most on Grand Cayman), and along with native cooking, there are Chinese, Thai, Japanese, Mexican, Indian, Italian, French, British, Spanish, Brazilian, Cuban, American, Middle Eastern, and African cuisines. Restaurants range from casual seaside settings to elegant luxury, and fine wines are on most menus.

The following restaurant price guide is for the average cost of a full meal with a glass of wine or beer:
  $ = under US$20
  $$ = US$20–40
  $$$ = above US$40

Grand Cayman

Bacchus
George Town
Tel: 949 5747
Popular haunt with the after-work crowd. Stay for dinner and chef/owner Keith Griffiths will tantalize your taste buds with such delights as the Salonika platter that includes a selection of Greek goodies such as chicken kebabs, hummus, olives, and pitta bread. $$–$$$

Breezes by the Bay Tropical Grill and Rhum Deck
Harbour Drive, George Town
Tel: 949 8439
Dine on the balcony at this two-story casual restaurant and bar. Perfect for a bountiful lunch with dishes such as coconut shrimp, spicy lime marinated salad, and callallo soup made with spicy island greens. Fabulous views of the bay, great place to watch the sunset. $

Café Mediterraneo
Galleria Plaza, Seven Mile Beach
Tel: 949 8669
Salads include a refreshing *insalata di mare* (a mixed seafood salad), and an arugula salad

Above: conch fritters are among the most typical, and delicious, of Cayman Island foods with lemon vinaigrette topped with Parma ham. Try the classic lasagne or the fresh pistachio-encrusted snapper. $$

Casa Havana
Inside the Westin Casuarina Resort,
Seven Mile Beach
Tel: 945 3800
Heralded as the only AAA four-star restaurant in the Cayman Islands, this supremely elegant place received an award from *Wine Spectator* magazine and was deemed one of the best restaurants in the world for wine connoisseurs. The menu features classic Cuban dishes with a sophisticated flair, and tropical seafood specialties utilizing exotic fruits and vegetables. $$$

Castaways Grille
Grand Harbour, Red Bay
Tel: 947 3456
www.castawaysgrille.com
The perfect spot to enjoy a relaxed lunch or dinner either in air-conditioned comfort or on the restaurant's covered patio. Wine tasting takes place every Thursday evening. A red and white from the tasting then features on the evening fixed menu. Enjoy a great selection of French pastries and home-made breads next door at Café Grande. $$

Copper Kettle and Daily Grind Corita's
Central George Town
Tel: 949 2696
If you are hungry for breakfast venture upstairs to the Daily Grind to enjoy some of the best coffees in Cayman, along with a pastry or bagel, all served up by Mark

McTaggart, who is also a drummer for local bands. Downstairs Corita's Copper Kettle serves traditional Cayman fare. Take out or eat in ackee and codfish, liver and onions or fritters with everything. American breakfasts are also served. $

DJ's Cantina
Coconut Place, Seven Mile Beach
Tel: 945 4234
A lively and casual Mexican cantina with generous margaritas, and dishes such as shrimp tortillas, guacamole, burritos, and red-hot salsa. $$

Edoardo's
Coconut Place, Seven Mile Beach
Tel: 945 4408
Edoardo's has been serving authentic Italian cuisine in its cozy and welcoming restaurant for the past 18 years. Owners Raffaele Dell'Oglio and Dennis Rowe will make you feel like part of the family. Prince Edward Isle mussels are a popular choice. $$–$$$

Every Bloomin' Thing's Victorian Tea Room
Crewe Road, George Town
Tel: 945 1701
A great escape from the hustle of Downtown, this tranquil and soothing tearoom in the eastern reaches of the capital is a popular hang-out for local people who come for the wide assortment of teas, coffees, and the delicious homemade scones, cakes, pies, soups, and sandwiches. $

Full of Beans
Pasadora Place, George Town
Tel: 943 2326
Tucked away behind the front of Pasadora Place lies this café-cum-restaurant. Mosaics on the wall and a cool and contemporary design complement the Asian-infused cuisine. Owner Cindy Butler places firm emphasis on the freshest ingredients. The Thai chicken wrap is always a winner with drizzlings of peanut and hot pepper sauces on the side. $

Gateway to India
West Bay Road, Seven Mile Beach
Tel: 946 2815
With a rich decor that includes tapestries

Left: there is no shortage of places to enjoy a casual lunch and artifacts, this restaurant imports its spices from India, and includes authentic specialty items such as shrimp Masala on a crispy rice *dosa*, vegetable samosas, mint coriander chutney, and an array of curry dishes. $$

Grand Old House
South Church Street, George Town
Tel: 949 9333
This enduring restaurant in a stately Caribbean Great House (dating to 1908) is a local legend that is often used for island weddings and lavish balls. Before coming to Grand Cayman, resident chef Kandathil Mathai cooked for royalty and politicians such as Prince Charles, Margaret Thatcher, and Ronald Reagan. Featuring European and New World cuisine in dishes such as tenderloin black Angus beef, potato-crusted tuna, and lobster sauteed with shallots, it also has impeccable service and an extensive wine list. Reservations recommended. $$$

Kaibo Yacht Club & Restaurant
Water Cay Road, Cayman Kai
Tel: 947 9975
Overlooking the sleepy shores of Kaibo Beach, this elegant dining spot has an eclectic blend of Caribbean and New Orleans cuisine. From classic Caymanian fish dishes to spicy seafood gumbos, crawfish stew, and jambalaya. Reservations suggested. $$$

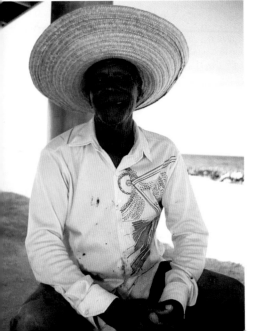

Liberty Restaurant
Rev. Blackman Road, West Bay
Tel: 949 3226
The comfortable Liberty caters to families, with seafood specialties and a children's menu that includes burgers and fries, chicken fingers, turtle stew, curried goat, and lemon meringue pie. $$

Mezza Restaurant and Bar
West Bay Road, Seven Mile Beach
Tel: 946 3992
The expanded Mezza tends to attract the 30 plus crowd out for an evening of sophisticated but relaxed dining. Partners Guy and Alex work their customers with panache. Bendable lights and glass brickwork make for a contemporary and trendy location. $$–$$$

Portofino Wreck View
Colliers Road, East End
Tel: 947 2700
This restaurant caters to a mixture of local people and tourists. A fine Italian eatery it is well known for its great service and traditional Italian dishes, such as veal *scaloppini*, lasagne, seafood pasta, antipasto, and garlic bread. $$

Ristorante Pappagallo
Conch Point Road, West Bay
Tel: 949 1119
With a thatch-palm roof and a wooden bridge over a secluded lagoon, this eatery is constructed out of bamboo, local stones, and marble. Surrounding the property is a 14-acre (5.5-ha) bird sanctuary, and inside are dozens of caged macaws, cockatoos, and African gray parrots. The menu features Northern Italian cuisine with homemade pastas, foccacia, seafood dishes, and dessert pastries. $$$

Thai Orchid
Queens Court, Seven Mile Beach
Tel: 949 7955
In a small shopping center, this classic Thai eatery has chefs from Bangkok who effortlessly whip up satay, bean thread noodle soup, pad Thai, crispy duck in ginger sauce, vegetable curry, and sauteed shrimp with bamboo shoots. $$

Left: local in a beach-side café

The Brasserie
Cricket Square, George Town
Tel: 945 1815
Contemporary colonial decor makes for elegant yet relaxed surroundings. Popular with business people because of its central location, The Brasserie has a dedicated regular list of lunchtime patrons in particular, who enjoy the best seafood and pasta dishes, often with an Asian kick. If duck appears on the menu, it should be sampled. $$–$$$

The Lobster Pot
North Church Street, George Town
Tel: 949 2736
Labeled 'Cayman's favorite seafood restaurant by the sea', the Lobster Pot was completely refurbished to its original pre-Hurricane Ivan decor and offers superb views over the ocean as well as great martinis and daiquiris. $$

Ye Olde English Bakery and Tea Room
Corner of Mary Street, George Town
Tel: 945 2420
Quintessentially English, they make a great cup of tea here, along with tempting pastries such as sausage rolls, jam doughnuts, and custard tarts. Buy home-made bread and rolls or enjoy a bacon bap and brown sauce. $

Cayman Brac

Almond Tree Café
Mac Plaza, Spot Bay
Tel: 948 0372
Owner Julie Ann McLaughlin does the home-style cooking in this small and friendly place and serves heaped portions for lunch and dinner that include oxtail soup, fried fish, curried chicken, beef stew, saltfish and ackee, pepper steak, and meat patties – unmissable delicious Caribbean flavors. Warm, charming, and delightful to talk to, Miss McLaughlin on occasion even catches the fish herself. The café also has burgers and hot dogs. $

Aunt Sha's Kitchen
Dennis Point, South Side
Tel: 948 1587
Open seven days a week, this indoor/outdoor restaurant doubles as a late-night pool hall, and features a combination Caymanian/Chinese menu that includes sweet and sour chicken, chop suey, grilled lobster, fried fish, and lemon pie. $

Captain's Table
West End, near Brac Caribbean Beach Resort
Tel: 948 1418
An elegant, air-conditioned restaurant with candlelight and linen tablecloths. Its broad menu includes steaks, burgers, chicken, and several seafood pasta dishes. $$

La Esperanza Restaurant
Stake Bay, at La Esperanza Hotel
Tel: 948 0531
Al fresco dining by the sea doesn't get any better in the Brac than at this relaxed spot, that is truly away from it all. Portions are huge and the menu includes island-style dishes featuring the catch-of-the-day, such as conch steaks, turtle, shrimp and lobster. The owner, Bussy's, weekend barbecues on Friday and Saturday nights are legendary. Free transportation provided.

Little Cayman

Birds of Paradise Restaurant
At Little Cayman Beach Resort
Tel: 948 1033
Located at Little Cayman Beach Resort, this buffet-style restaurant caters to hotel guests and the public, with a good and diverse selection of appetizing salads and entrees, as well as puddings such as Key Lime pie. Voted 'Top Restaurant' by the readers of *Rodale's Scuba Diving* magazine.

Hungry Iguana
Iguana Court, near Paradise Villas
Tel: 948 0007
Named for an iguana known to roam nearby, this large, modern, seaside eatery features breakfast buffets, and lunches and dinners that include fish sandwiches, burgers, salads, steaks, and prime rib. $

Southern Cross Club
South Hole Sound
Tel: 948 1099
A pleasant spot featuring gourmet Caymanian and American-style dishes. $$$

NIGHTLIFE

Evenings in the Cayman Islands begin with a wonderful piece of free entertainment – looking for the rare green flash, a natural ray of green light that dances briefly on the horizon as the sun gently slips into the Caribbean Sea. Look for it on clear, dry days.

When darkness sets in, the nights are marked by reggae, wafting from bars, lively steel-band performances, and dancing under the stars. Also on hand, on Grand Cayman, are comedy clubs, community theater acts, dance troupes, discos, and dinner cruises.

In Cayman Brac and Little Cayman, the majority of evening entertainment is staged by the hotels, and consists mostly of hotel-hosted beach barbecues, dance parties, and casual after-diving cocktails by the pool.

The legal drinking age is 18, and this is taken seriously – identification is often checked at the door. There are, of course, laws governing drinking and driving, and these, as well as plain common sense, mean that taxi services are recommended for all premeditated bacchanalia.

As required by local law, all bars and nightclubs close at 1am on weekdays and at midnight on Saturday and Sunday. Although many bars are open, there is no live music or entertainment on Sunday. A local entertainments' guide called *What's Hot Cayman*, offers current news about nightlife on the island and is available free at most hotels.

Although evening entertainment shuts down early there is still lots of fun to be had.

Whether you want to have a quiet drink, or dance your socks off, it's all here.

Bars/Nightclubs

Aqua Beach

West Bay Road
Tel: 946 6398
A casual dining restaurant and bar favored by the young, lively and gorgeous crowd who then want to dance the night away at the neighboring Next Level nightclub. Enjoy intimate seating or join in with the crowds.

Bamboo

West Bay Road, Seven Mile Beach
Tel: 949 1234
Popular with an upscale Cayman crowd, this sophisticated sushi bar and lounge is the place to be, especially on Friday night. Dress for cocktails not the beach. The bar has a selection of sake and wine by the glass.

Club Chameleon

West Bay Road, Seven Mile Beach
Tel: 943 2582
A different musical treat every night at the island's largest nightclub. Two-stories with sleek white decor complete with a martini bar and state-of-the-art sound system. Caribbean music on Friday and country and western on Saturday. Call ahead to see what's happening.

Club Inferno

West Bay, Hell
Tel: 949 3263
What else would a club in Hell be called?

Live Caribbean, Latin, and country music with a down-home local atmosphere, right next door to the Hell Post Office.

Coconut Joe's
West Bay Road
Tel: 949 5637
www.coconutjoes.com.ky
Casual outdoor dining with live music and a large-screen TV. The place has a beach house-style set up.

Country & Western Bar
Red Bay Road
Tel: 945 9335
Definitely one for the locals, the Country & Western bar plays music of that ilk, as you would expect, but also serves up cracking good local food, such as conch (pronounced 'conk') fritters, curried goat, and spicy stewed chicken.

Fidel Murphy's
West Bay Road, Seven Mile Beach
Tel: 949 5189
Although it's hard to imagine such a thing, an 'Irish' Fidel Castro is the theme of this lively saloon that features tall drinks, Cuban cigars, and live music on weekends.

Hammerheads
North Church Street, George Town
Tel: 949 3080
Located on the George Town waterfront, Hammerheads was one of the first bars to be up and running following Hurricane Ivan and has retained a faithful band of patrons. Everything has a unique island flair, from the Old Dutch beer brewed on the premises to the menu that includes turtle stew and fresh seafood caught by local fishermen. The inmates at Cayman's Northward Prison crafted the sign above the entrance.

Hard Rock Café
Church Street, George Town
Tel: 945 2020
Starting off with a bustling singles scene at happy hour, this chain, known for its music memorabilia and potent drinks, continues to party well into the night, and has a Caribbean island theme that includes an old acoustic guitar once owned by singer Jimmy Buffett.

Lone Star Bar & Grill
West Bay Road, Seven Mile Beach
Tel: 945 5175
Rated one of the 'top 100 bars in the world' by *Newsweek* magazine, this American-style sports-theme saloon attracts beer-drinking dive masters, bourbon-drinking bankers, and a slew of tourists drinking all kinds of things.

Matrix
Seven Mile Beach, West Bay Road
Tel: 949 7169
One of the island's most popular nightclubs among locals and visitors alike, Matrix delivers high-tech/high-energy dance music. The club is well appointed with the latest in audio and visual technology. The large bar and comfortable seating surrounds a massive dance floor. Dress is smart-casual.

Ports of Call Bar
West Bay Road, George Town
Tel: 949 7729
Tucked inside the Wharf Restaurant complex, the Ports of Call is a romantic, waterfront hideaway that is very popular with couples. Its nightly live music ranges from Paraguayan harpists to slow-moving dance tunes.

Rackam's Pub at Calico Jack's
North Church Street, George Town
Tel: 945 3860
Perfectly located for watching the sun go

Left: eating outdoors on a balmy evening is one of the joys of the Cayman Islands
Above: beginning an evening at the Cayman Kai Resort.

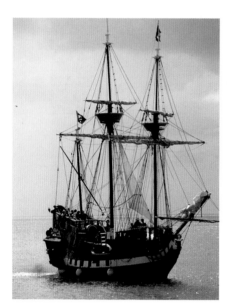

join in), and a fire eater (participation not recommended).

Sunset House My Bar
South Church Street, George Town
Tel: 949-7111
This large, open-air bar with a thatched-roof is located by the seaside and is especially popular with scuba divers. Weekend domino games attract a local crowd. Occasional water-themed movies and lectures with colorful slide shows on the outdoor wall. Visitors can enjoy reasonably-priced drinks and a British dish of tasty fish and chips.

The Next Level Nightclub and Lounge
West Bay Road, Seven Mile Beach
Tel: 949 7169
A strobe lights and glittering disco ball kind of place that has a jam-packed dance floor on weekends. With some of the best DJs on Grand Cayman spinning the discs, the entertainment here ranges from American rock and hip-hop to trendy techno and Euro-style dance nights.

Dance/Choral/Theater

Cayman Islands National Dance Company
Savannah, Grand Cayman
Tel: 947 6616
Also known as Dance Unlimited, this local troupe of 20 dancers founded in 1988 by Jamaica School of Dance graduate, Lorna Reid, offers a week-long spring season (the month varies each year) and a two-day

down, Rackam's is popular with the Friday night crowd who enjoy mixing after a hard day's work. The bar's cocktails are always popular as are the usual menu favorites, such as cheeseburgers and stir fries. Enjoy being sprayed by a cool mist of vapor that intermittently emits from the bar.

Rum Point Bar & Restaurant
Rum Point, Grand Cayman
Tel: 947 9412
These days, this bar is where George Novak, the legendary 'barefoot man' of Grand Cayman, plays several nights a week. About 20 years ago, Novak sang his original songs barefoot in the sand on Seven Mile Beach and now he's virtually a local institution. With a blend of calypso, reggae, soca, and country music, his act is definitely worth seeking out.

Stingers
Seven Mile Beach, West Bay Road
Tel: 945 3000
Located poolside at the Comfort Suites Hotel, Stingers restaurant and bar offers the perfect spot for casual dining. There is a Caribbean Luau every Wednesday and Saturday beginning at 6.30pm with buffet all-you-can-eat dining, a live dance band, limbo dancer (patrons are encouraged to

Above: what could be nicer than a dinner cruise on the Jolly Roger as the sun sets over the islands? **Right**: Stingray beer, the islands local brew

Christmas show. Held at both the Harquail Theatre and the Prospect Playhouse, the performances are a diverse array of African, West Indian, modern, and ballet styles.

Cayman National Choir
Grand Cayman
Tel: 949 7800
Local musicians, along with visiting US musicians, perform with this company during a Spring Music Festival in May, and a classic Christmas production in December at various locations on Grand Cayman.

Harquail Theatre
West Bay Road, Seven Mile Beach
Tel: 949 5054
Managed by the Cayman Drama Society, this small theater stages five major productions each year. They include works created by Caymanian and West Indian playwrights and range from comedies to dramas and musicals. It also offers intimate dinner and theater shows on Friday nights.

Prospect Playhouse
Red Bay, Grand Cayman
Tel: 949 5477
A 330-seat community theater that hosts local drama, comedy, and musical productions, visiting stage shows, art exhibits, and theatrical workshops.

Dinner Cruises
Jolly Roger Dinner Cruise
Bayside Dock, South Terminal, George Town
Tel: 945 7245
This replica of a 17th-century galleon sets sail most evenings at dusk for a romantic dinner cruise that is very popular among honeymooners and young couples. Along with a glorious sunset and the peaceful ride, the cruise includes rum punch, and a full dinner with wine.

Red Sail Sunset Cruises
Seven Mile Beach
Tel: 945 5965
Operating from sites at both Seven Mile Beach and Rum Point, Red Sail runs two-hour sunset cruises with cocktails and appetizers, and dinner cruises with three-course meals.

Cinema
Cinema I & II
West Bay Road, George Town
Tel: 949 4011
Although there are numerous video rental stores throughout the Cayman Islands, there is only one movie theater – and this is it. With a double screen, it offers current American films Monday through Saturday nights. The cinema is currently undergoing major refurbishment due to damage caused by Hurricane Ivan.

Above: live music in the bars and clubs

CALENDAR OF EVENTS

Scattered throughout the year, several vibrant festivals take place in the Cayman Islands. Mostly held outdoors, they are joyous, colorful spectacles, many of which pay tribute to the islands' maritime and cultural heritage. The following is a brief list.

February

mid-February: a kaleidoscope of vivid purple and pink sets the mood at the Queen Elizabeth II Botanic Park, when it pays tribute to the tropical glory of the island with the annual **Orchid Show**. With heady scents filling the air, there are orchid displays, horticultural lectures and discussions, orchid-growing demonstrations, and exotic plants for sale. Tel: 947 9462.

late February: the pre-Lenten frenzy of the **Mardi Gras** festival stirs up the tiny island of Little Cayman and the entire community takes part in the festivities. As the 40 days of Lent are tied to Easter, the exact date varies from year to year. Along with naming a king and queen, the annual island-style jump-up includes elaborate float parades, costume contests (some of the costumes are quite extraordinary), street dances, live music, fireworks over the water, and, of course, plenty of rum. Tel: 948 1010.

March/April

early March: the **Cayman Islands National Trust Gala** is an elegant, black-tie affair in George Town with gourmet foods, fine wines and live music. The gala's mission is to raise funds for the preservation of the island's natural environment as well as places of historic significance. Tel: 949 0121.

March 17: the **St Patrick's Day Jog** on Grand Cayman was inaugurated by Caymanian descendants of Irish settlers. Beginning and ending at the Britannia Golf Course (tel: 949 8020), the 5K-run (3 miles/5km) awards several prizes to both winners and losers.

mid- to late March: the waters off Grand Cayman come alive with the **Round the Island Regatta**. Organised by the Cayman Islands Sailing Club, it is one of the more competitive races in the Caribbean. This four-day race and on-shore party includes

crafts ranging from small dinghies to sleek 80-ft (24-m) catamarans. Tel: 947 7913.

late March to mid-April: an annual **Easter Bash** is held in Little Cayman that includes food and festivities and an auction of arts and crafts to benefit the Little Cayman National Trust.

mid-April: the culture and arts extravaganza known as **Cayfest** envelopes the island of Grand Cayman for several days and means plenty of live music, drama, dance, and arts and crafts displays. There are also special children's activities, fun-packed festival days, boat launches and regattas, and a real party atmosphere, with local food and drink on sale. Tel: 949 5938.

In conjunction with the Grand Cayman event, Cayman Brac hosts its own **Cayfest Seaside Regatta** with both sailing and power boats taking part.

May/June

early May: the **Cayman Islands International Fishing Tournament** attracts keen anglers from all over the world to compete in several categories. Along with cash prizes and trophies, participating fishermen and women always go home with tall tales of big fish, which are often as enjoyable in the re-telling as they were at the time.

throughout May: for those who look to the green for fun, a couple of the golf tournaments on the May docket include the annual **Cayman Islands Chamber of Commerce Golf Classic**, and the **Cinco de Mayo Corona Golf Tournament** at the Links.

Above: island flowers: the annual National Trust Gala raises money for the preservation of flora and fauna as well as places of historic interest

late May: the yearly **Batabano Carnival** (pronounced *bata-banoo*) comes to downtown George Town. Featuring classic carnival music and live calypso and soca bands, the annual jubilee is also noted for its array of concession stands offering tasty tidbits of Caymanian and Caribbean cuisine, a large float parade, plenty of costumed merrymakers, and street dances. There is an attractive prize for the best costume in the parade, but only outfits made in the Cayman Islands are eligible for the competition.

July

early July: island-style cuisine is the theme of the popular annual fete known as the **Taste of Cayman**, hosted by the local restaurant association. Turtle stew, Caymanian fish, conch fritters and chowders are among the many treats, as well as the ubiquitous, rich and potent rum cake. Tel: 949 8522.

mid-July: the hard-fought **Governor's Cup** sailing challenge takes place. The waters around Grand Cayman are jam-packed with sophisticated racing teams from all over the world as well as local favorites, as fans cheer them on from the beaches and bars. Also in mid-July, **Family Week** is held on Cayman Brac with special activities such as kids' water sports available, as well as well-priced vacation packages for families.

September/October

mid-September: **Cayman Madness Dive Vacation** lures divers from around the world for a week of underwater treasure hunts, beach parties, live concerts, and prizes.

late October: Blackbeard and his buccaneers come to town during **Pirates' Week Festival**, when all three islands take part in the rousing revelry. Without a doubt the grandest event in the Cayman Islands, this yearly bash includes a mock invasion of the George Town harbor, complete with costumed pirates. Also part of the program are an underwater treasure hunt, children's games and rides, jazz and reggae concerts, food fairs, cultural heritage displays, golf tournaments, teen disco parties, dance and costume contests, a 3 miles/5km run, and firework displays. It's all in honor of the Cayman Islands' maritime heritage. Events can actually run for up to 10 days.

Right: pirates on parade in the October Pirates' Week Festival

November

early November: Seven Mile Beach is the location of the **Annual Turtle Release**, when hundreds of turtles from the Cayman Turtle Farm are released back to the wild. The green sea turtles, an endangered species, are born and reared on the farm in Grand Cayman as part of a breed-and-release program. So far more than 30,000 turtles have been returned to the Caribbean Sea and divers regularly report sightings of the creatures. Visitors and local people turn out to witness the event. Tel: 949 3894

December

The annual **Jazz Festival** held early in December at Pageant Beach, has seen big-name attractions, such as Roberta Flack, performing on stage.

The Christmas spirit sets the tone for December, of course, and traditional holiday celebrations fill the air throughout the month. Home-owners on all the Cayman islands compete in the annual **Christmas House Lighting Contest** and the result is spectacular display of twinkling lights, illuminated Santas, and even a few reindeer complete with sunglasses. There are also seasonal evenings of carol singing on the steps of the George Town Courthouse, tree-lighting ceremonies, and a Santa Claus Landing Party for the children.

Practical
Information

GETTING THERE

By Air

Several airlines offer regularly scheduled flights to Grand Cayman from the US, UK, Jamaica, Honduras, and Cuba. From Miami, there are more than 45 direct flights a week to Grand Cayman and the flight time is 1 hour 20 minutes. Grand Cayman's Owen Roberts International Airport (tel: 949 7733), which receives over 100 flights per week, is a modern facility with fast and efficient service that includes a helpful tourist information desk.

Cayman Airways offers flights from Grand Cayman to Cayman Brac and Little Cayman, via its Cayman Airways Express service. The airline also operates a 737 jet service between Grand Cayman and Cayman Brac. Island Air also has flights from Grand Cayman to both Cayman Brac and Little Cayman.

When departing the Cayman Islands, visitors are required to pay a departure tax of US$25 per person (if not included in the air fare) and to check in for their flights at least 1½ hours prior to departure. No departure taxes are charged for inter-island travel within the Cayman Islands.

By Sea

The Cayman Islands guards against congestion and overcrowding by allowing no more than four large cruise ships to sail into port at any one time. Several companies regularly sail to Grand Cayman, including: Carnival, Celebrity, Crown Commodore, Costa, Cunard, Dolphin, Holland America, Norwegian, Princess, Royal Caribbean, Seabourn, Seven Seas, and Sun Line. Most of these companies begin their tours in Miami, Fort Lauderdale, or San Juan.

Ships are required to anchor offshore and use tenders to ferry their passengers to either the North or the South Dock Terminals in George Town. Situated fairly close together, both terminals are within easy walking

distance of the many restaurants, visitor attractions, and shopping centers in downtown George Town.

The Cayman Islands is also an extremely popular port of call for privately owned sailboats and yachts, and many marinas throughout the islands offer moorings for rent by the day or the week. There is no ferry service connecting the three Cayman Islands.

TRAVEL ESSENTIALS

When to Visit

The most popular time to visit the Cayman Islands is mid-December through mid-April. It is also the most expensive when it comes to hotel rates. This is also the busiest time of year for cruise ships in the Caribbean.

The summer season of July and August means family vacation time for many, so these months bring a boost in visitor arrivals. And in the past few years, the Cayman Islands has promoted itself as a spring-break destination, when college students from across the US descend upon Grand Cayman.

The 'shoulder' seasons of spring and fall are the quietest and least-expensive times of all. The one exception, however, is during the late October Pirates' Week Festival when all three islands are packed with tourists, and hotel rooms are booked many months in advance.

Left: a cruise ship dwarfs a traditional-style galleon
Above Right: the Angel of the Ocean keeps watch over the port

GETTING ACQUAINTED

Geography

Situated about 20 degrees north of the equator in the crystal-clear Caribbean Sea, the three coral atoll islands that make up the Cayman Islands are 150 miles (242km) south of Cuba, 480 miles (772km) south of Miami, and 180 miles (290km) northwest of Jamaica.

The largest and most developed is Grand Cayman (population approximately 42,500; pronounced *kay-món*) at 22 miles (35km) long and 4 miles (6.5km) wide. Cayman Brac (population 1,600) is 12 miles (19km) long by a little over 1 mile (1.6km) wide. And Little Cayman (population 120) is 10 miles (16km) long and 1 mile (1.6km) wide.

Except for the bluff on Cayman Brac that rises to 140ft (43m), the islands are relatively flat, with no mountains or rivers. Their interiors are solid limestone and mostly covered in dense woodlands. Beneath the sea, however, the terrain is a dramatic expanse of submarine mountain outcrops. Between the Cayman Islands and nearby Jamaica is the Cayman Trough, also called the Cayman Trench, with the deepest point (25,000ft/7,620m) in the Caribbean Sea.

Population

Native-born people are called Caymanians. One-third of the population is foreign-born (mostly American, British, and Jamaican citizens), and over 100 nationalities are pre-

sent. The majority of Caymanians, however, are multiracial descendants of early English, Irish, Scottish, Welsh, and African settlers. Because the islands were never a major slave colony, and because many foreigners came here as seafarers, there is a great deal of ethnic and racial tolerance among the residents.

Government and Economy

The Cayman Islands is a British Overseas Territory led by a governor, an appointee of the Queen. The governor leads the Executive Council, which includes three official and five elected ministers. Offshore finance and tourism are the mainstays of the local economy, providing local people with the highest standard of living in the Caribbean.

Religion/How Not to Offend

In general, Caymanians are conservative, respectful, and religious people. There is a slight formality in the way they interact with each other; people are introduced as Mr, Mrs or Miss, and manners are always of the utmost importance.

There are over 75 churches, and Sunday is devoted to prayer and family. Over 90 percent of the population are Christian, with the Anglican Church and Seventh-Day Adventists being the most common denominations.

There are no nudist beaches; public nudity and topless bathing are prohibited by law.

Language

The official language of the Cayman Islands is English. The Caymanian accent is delight-

Above: inter-island flights utilize small, propeller-powered planes ful to the ear, and includes intonations from Scottish, Irish, Welsh, and Cornish accents.

Visas and Passports

All visitors (including cruise-ship passengers) are required to possess a current passport as well as a return plane ticket. US, Canadian, and most European citizens can enter the Cayman Islands without a visa and are allowed to stay for up to six months. People of other nationalities need to check with their government for current requirements.

Upon arrival, immigration forms must be completed. A copy of the form is stamped by officials and you must keep it until leaving the Cayman Islands.

Work permit requirements are very strict, and require a great deal of government paperwork in advance. In George Town, the immigration office can be found at the Government Administration Building on Elgin Avenue.

Vaccinations

No vaccinations are required.

Customs

Upon arrival, all visitors must pass through customs and declare all items of value, such as cameras and jewelry. The duty-free allowance when entering the Cayman Islands is approximately 2 pints (1 liter) of liquor or 7 pints (4 liters) of wine, and 200 cigarettes or 50 cigars. Plants, flowers, fruits, vegetables, and many food products are not allowed into the islands.

The possession of illegal drugs can lead to imprisonment as well as fines, and suitcases are opened and searched at the airport on occasion. The possession of firearms is also illegal.

Upon departure, US citizens are allowed to return home with up to US$400-worth of purchases without paying duty. Turtle products such as shells or canned meat cannot be taken into the US or through the US while in transit to other countries.

Weather

The Cayman Islands has a tropical climate that varies only slightly throughout the year. The average temperature range is 78–92°F (25–33°C) in summer and 68–82°F (20–28°C) in winter. Annual rainfall averages about 68 inches (173cm) a year. The islands are usually cooled off in the afternoon by showers during the rainy season (May through October), and in winter delightful sea breezes are constant. Trade winds, usually blowing from the east, are prevalent.

The hurricane season runs from June through November, and a major storm can wreak havoc. The islands are well prepared, however, and modern hotels have been built to withstand winds of severe magnitude. In case of a serious threat, an evacuation plan goes into effect, and tourists are asked to leave the island. Storms are monitored regularly, with updates reported on local radio and television, especially during a hurricane 'watch' or 'warning' period. The Cayman Islands Hurricane Hotline can be reached on all three islands by calling tel: 946 3333.

The most memorable storm in recent history was Hurricane Ivan in 2004. The category 4/5 storm passed by the south coast of Grand Cayman inflicting severe damage on parts of the island. South Sound, Prospect, Bodden Town, and East End coastal properties were particularly badly hit, although it is estimated that 90 percent of all buildings on the island were damaged. However, rebuilding was swift.

The temperature of the sea remains warm (75–85°F/24–29°C) throughout most of the year except for a month or two in winter. Surface waves are usually larger and more powerful on the windward side of the islands.

Clothing

With a year-round tropical climate, casual summer clothing is always worn in the Cayman Islands. Except for a few of the finer restaurants, where jackets for men are suggested, a crisp, shirt is all that is expected.

Shorts, tank tops, and sandals are commonly worn by both sexes. Bathing costumes, however, are unacceptable in commercial establishments and should be reserved for beaches, boats, and resort areas.

Sun hats are a must, especially in summer, and sunglasses are suggested. It is wise to take an umbrella with you for sudden downpours, especially in the afternoon during the summer months. The sand can get very hot so sandals are a good idea. Smart, resort-casual is the best way to describe the dress in most nightclubs and restaurants. A sweater, light jacket, or shawl for the evenings is suggested, since many establishments run their air conditioning full blast to reduce the temperature.

Electricity

The current is 120 volts and standard US flat-pin plugs are used. Electrical appliances made in the US do not need adapters, but most European-made ones do. Power cuts are rare.

Time Zone

The Cayman Islands operate on Eastern Standard Time which is the same as the time in New York and five hours behind GMT. Between April and October they are one hour behind EST.

MONEY MATTERS

Currency

The official currency is the Cayman Island dollar, usually fixed at a rate of CI$1 to US$1.20. Bills are issued in units of $100, $50, $25, $10, $5, and $1. US dollars are accepted everywhere in the islands so American visitors need not change their currency before a trip.

Banking/Cash Machines/ Currency Exchange

Although there are over 500 banks licensed in the Cayman Islands, there are only a few retail banks that are licensed to undertake transactions with the public. They include Butterfield Bank, Scotiabank, FirstCaribbean International Bank, Cayman National Bank and Royal Bank of Canada. Most are open Mon–Fri 9am–4pm, except on Little Cayman where the sole bank is open only on Wednesday. The banks all offer a fixed rate of exchange that rarely varies. Most large hotels also offer exchange services. There is no black market. Cash machines (ATMs) are abundant and are located at banks, grocery

stores, and shopping centers throughout the three islands.

Credit Cards

While a few small vendors will only take cash, the majority of businesses accept credit cards. Most establishments post a list of the cards they will accept; this usually includes MasterCard, Visa, American Express, Diners Club, and Discover.

Tipping

Tipping at the rate of 15 percent is common in most restaurants and some include the gratuity on the bill, so check before adding it. Although tips to taxi drivers, baggage handlers, and maids are welcome, locals in general are not at all demanding when it comes to tips. Bell hops and airport baggage handlers customarily get $1 to $2 per bag.

Departure Tax

Most airlines add the price of the Cayman Islands Government departure tax to the price of the ticket. If not, a fee of US$25 is collected at the airport. This fee is included in the price of most cruises.

GETTING AROUND

Rental Cars

The Cayman Islands are easy to get around and driving is simple and safe. Except for George Town and the Seven Mile Beach area of Grand Cayman, there is very little traffic. Driving is on the left and most rental cars have automatic transmissions. Rates are very reasonable and the service is hassle-free. The purchase of a local driving permit is required by law and costs US$12. Cars, jeeps, and vans are all available. Drivers must be at least 18, have a valid driver's license, and a credit card. Among the car rental firms are:

Grand Cayman: Andy's (tel: 949 8111), Budget (tel: 949 5605), Cico (tel: 949 2468), Coconut (tel: 949 4377/4037), Economy (tel: 949 9550 or 949 8992), Hertz (tel: 949 2280), and Soto's (tel: 945 2424).

Cayman Brac: Brac Rent-a-Car (tel: 948 1515), B & S Motors (tel: 948 1646), Four Ds (tel: 948 0459).

Little Cayman: McLaughlin (tel: 948 1000).

Above: Caymanian heraldic symbol

Taxis

Taxis in Grand Cayman are not metered. There are fixed fares from the airport, with extra charges for large pieces of luggage and more than four passengers. Taxis can also be hired for local transportation and guided tours. A minimum fee of CI$4 for the first mile (1.6km) is the rule. Taxis can be found at the airport, major hotels, and most public places around Grand Cayman. A few useful numbers are:

Grand Cayman: Ace (tel: 777 7777), Charlie's Super Cab (tel: 888 8888/ 916 6590), Webster's (tel: 945 1433).

Cayman Brac: Most hotels on the island provide local transportation, but it's best to rent a car to get around.

Little Cayman: Most hotels on the island provide local transportation.

Public Transportation

A regular public bus system finally came to Grand Cayman in 1998 and works relatively well. The main terminal is near the Public Library on Edward Street in George Town and there are eight routes around the island that go to West Bay, Bodden Town, East End, and North Side. One-way fares are about CI$2, and the buses operate daily from 6am to 11pm. For more information, tel: 945 5100.

Ferry

There is no ferry service connecting the three islands but the reliable and fun *Rum Pointer* Ferry, a 120-passenger vessel, usually runs back and forth to Rum Point from Grand Cayman's Hyatt Regency Hotel (tel: 949 9098) several times a day. The cost is US$15 for the round-trip and reservations are suggested.

The *Rum Pointer* ferry was badly damaged during Hurricane Ivan, but was to be quickly repaired and back in operation transporting passengers.

Tour Operators

Several companies offer regular day-trip tours and specially designed tours.

Grand Cayman: Majestic Tours, tel: 949 7773, Reality Tours, tel: 947 7200, Reid's Premier Tours, tel: 945 3345.

Cayman Brac: D&M Tours, tel: 948 2307.

Right: there are quite a few stylish old American cars on the islands

HOURS AND HOLIDAYS

Business Hours

Stores and businesses usually open Mon–Sat 9am–5pm. Nearly all forms of commerce shut down on Sunday, including grocery stores, markets, and tourist gift shops.

Public Holidays

New Year's Day (1 January)
Ash Wednesday (date variable, depending on Easter)
Good Friday (date variable)
Easter Monday (date variable)
Discovery Day (third Monday in May)
Queen's Birthday (mid-June)
Constitution Day (first Monday in July)
Remembrance Day (second or third Monday in November)
Christmas Day (25 December)
Boxing Day (26 December)

ACCOMMODATION

Tourism is the backbone of the local economy, and the Cayman Islands are noted for modern accommodations, including over 5,000 'tourist rooms' that range from luxury hotels and condos to small inns and dive resorts. Because it caters to the mid- and upscale markets, bargain hotels are hard to find, but they do exist. Overall, the quality of service in most properties is excellent.

The government publishes an annual hotel rates and facts guide, available from the tourist board. There are also three helpful websites: www.caymanresorts.com, www.caymanislands.ky and www.caymanvillas.com. A government 'bed tax' of 10 percent is added to all hotel bills, and many properties also add a 10 percent service/gratuity charge as well.

Prices vary according to the time of year,

with winter months costing on average 40 percent more than summer. Rates for the hotels listed below are in US dollars and are based on a nightly, double-occupancy stay.

$$$$ = over $300
$$$ = between $200 and $300
$$ = between $100 and $200
$ = under $100

Please note that hotel facilities may be limited due to damage caused by Hurricane Ivan.

Grand Cayman
Beachcomber Condominiums
Seven Mile Beach
Tel: 945 4470
www.beachcomber1.com
In the center of Seven Mile Beach, this 24-unit, luxury condo has elegant two- and three-bedroom apartments. Ocean-side pool and water sports. $$$$

Britannia Hyatt Villas
Seven Mile Beach/Britannia Golf Course
Tel: 949 1234 or 800 233 1234
www.britanniavillas.com
Two- and three-bedroom units with elegant British colonial architecture and decor, fully equipped kitchens, and all amenities. Guests have access to the Hyatt Regency resort golf, pools, and 24-hour room service. $$$$

Cobalt Coast
Sea Fan Drive
Tel: 946 5656
www.cobaltcoast.com
A small, quiet oceanfront resort situated on the north shore, with its own dive experts on-site who can accommodate all your water sports needs. Swimming pool, but no beach on the property. Good hotel restaurant. $$–$$$

Comfort Suites
Seven Mile Beach
Tel: 945 7300
www.caymancomfort.com
Perfectly located hotel half-way up Seven Mile Beach with individual suites that serve basic needs; rooms have a refrigerator and a microwave. Enjoy evening meals around the pool at the hotel's popular restaurant. $$–$$$

Courtyard by Marriott
West Bay Road
Tel: 946 4433
www.marriott.com/gcmcy
Situated directly across from a beautiful stretch of Seven Mile Beach, the hotel has all of the necessary amenities including a restaurant and bar, its own pool and sunbathing area, and beachside facilities and water sports. $$–$$$

Driftwood Village
North Side
Tel: 947 9015
A private complex of four two-bedroom cottages – one available to rent – with kitchens, good fishing and diving from the shore. $$

Grapetree CocoPlum Condominiums
West Bay Road
Tel: 949 5959
www.caymancondos.com
Self-contained accommodation on Seven Mile Beach and steps away from restaurants, shopping, and water-sports. $$–$$$

Grand Cayman Marriott Beach Resort
West Bay Road
Tel: 949 0088 or 800 228 9290
www.marriott.com
Right on Seven Mile Beach, this lush state-of-the-art chain resort has lagoons, waterfalls, and stunning ocean views. The 300 guest rooms are luxurious; on-site amenities include a gym, Jacuzzi, tennis courts, water sports, dive shop, and restaurants. $$$$

Left: a traditional-style property on Cayman Brac

Hyatt Regency Grand Cayman Resort
Seven Mile Beach
Tel: 949 1234
www.hyatt.com
A sprawling, luxurious resort with every amenity. Includes plush beach-front villas and suites, a full-service spa, gym, tennis, children's activities, restaurants, bars, water sports, and golf. $$$$

Rum Run Villa
Cayman Kai
Tel: 945 4144
A pretty, two-bedroom villa on the beach, within walking distance of restaurants, tennis, and water sports. $$$

Spanish Bay Reef Resort
West Bay
Tel: 949 3765 or 800 482 3483
www.caymanresortsonline.com
An all-inclusive resort with a casual atmosphere, palm-lined beach and a coral reef within swimming distance. It has a freshwater pool, Jacuzzi, restaurant, bar, and scuba-diving instructors. All meals and use of a vehicle are included in the room rate. $$$

Sunset House
George Town
Tel: 949 7111 or 800 854 4767
www.sunsethouse.com
Heralded as a hotel for scuba divers run by scuba divers, this is a down-to-earth place with comfortable rooms, a restaurant, bar, freshwater pool, hot tub, and a full-service dive operation that offers scuba certifica-

tion classes, check-out dives, and advanced scuba training. $$

Wyndham Sunshine Suites
Seven Mile Beach
Tel: 949 3000
www.sunshinesuites.com
One of the few low-cost properties on Seven Mile Beach, with spacious rooms, kitchens, cable TV, and a pool. It's not on the ocean, but guests have access to the beach opposite. $$

Adam's Guest House
George Town
Tel: 949 2512
A friendly little inn in a private house with six air-conditioned rooms with private baths and kitchens. Walking distance of Downtown. $

Eldemire's Guest House
George Town
Tel: 949 5385
In a quiet neighborhood about 1 mile (1.6km) south of George Town, walking distance of Smith Cove, this 13-room inn has kitchen access, laundry, and private baths. $

Cayman Brac
Carib Sands
South Side West
Tel: 948 1121
www.caribsands.com
A modern, ocean-front complex with one- and two-bedroom apartments, a beautiful beach, water sports, restaurant, and bar. $$$

Above: elegant accommodations on Cayman Brac, seen from the air

Almond Beach Cottages
Spot Bay
Tel: 948 0667 or 800 972 9795
A small, luxurious three-unit property with spacious two-bedroom cottages, terraces and snorkeling just steps from the hotel. $$

Brac Reef Beach Resort
South Side West
Tel: 948 1323 or 800 327 3835
www.bracreef.com
A casual, relaxed dive resort set in 5 acres (0.5 ha) with a wide, white beach. Restaurant, bar, tennis, dock, gym, Jacuzzi, pool, photo lab, and full-service dive center. $$

Divi Tirara Beach Resort
South Side West
Tel: 948 1553
A casual two-story resort; private beach, freshwater pool, volleyball, tennis, and dive shop. $$

The Turtle Nest
Stake Bay
Tel: 948 1370
Fully furnished private house; sleeps four. Full-size kitchen and pool. $$

Walton's Mango Manor Guest House
Stake Bay
Tel: 948 0518
www.waltonsmangomanor.com
A small island-style getaway in a private home, with five rooms, private baths, laundry facilities, and breakfast included. $

Little Cayman
Conch Club Condominiums
Blossom Village
Tel: 948 1033 or 800 327 3835
Twelve plush, ocean-front two- and three-bedroom units; two pools, two docks, Jacuzzi, private beach, dive services. $$$

Pirates Point Resort
Preston Bay
Tel: 948 1010
Owned by award-winning chef, Gladys Howard, this delightful 10-room resort has a lively yet relaxed atmosphere, freshwater pool, full dive services, help-yourself-bar, and three gourmet meals a day. $$$

Little Cayman Beach Resort
Blossom Village
Tel: 948 1033 or 800 327 3835
www.littlecayman.com
Upscale dive resort with a full-service dive and photo shop, restaurant, bar, gym, and games room. $$

McCoy's Diving and Fishing Lodge
Bloody Bay
Tel: 948 0026 or 800 626 0496
A rustic eight-room lodge with a quaint atmosphere, freshwater pool, bar, restaurant, fishing, and diving facilities. $$

Suzy's Cottage
Blossom Village
Tel: 945 4144
A small beach-front cottage within walking distance of restaurants. It sleeps six and has a full kitchen and laundry facilities. $$

HEALTH/HYGIENE

The Cayman Islands pose no health threats to visitors other than sunburn, heat stroke, insect bites, and 'the bends' (the effects of decompression due to coming to the surface too quickly when scuba diving). Because of the ferocity of the sun, the use of sun-block lotion is strongly recommended at all times of the year. Mosquito repellent should be used when hiking in Cayman Brac and at Queen Elizabeth II Botanic Park in Grand Cayman.

To avoid heat stroke and dehydration, especially in summer, take shelter from the sun at midday, always wear a hat, and drink plenty of fresh water. Desalination plants provide clean tap water that is safe to drink, and bottled water is available on the islands. Public restrooms can be found at restaurants, visitor attractions, shopping centers, and banks.

Medical/Dental Services/ Pharmacies
It is advisable to take out private medical insurance to cover the costs of any emergency care. The government-run George Town Hospital (tel: 949 8600) has a 24-hour emergency room as well as a decompression chamber for scuba divers. Cayman Brac has the Faith Hospital (tel: 948 2243), and Little

Cayman has a small clinic (tel: 948 1051). Dialing 911 anywhere in the islands will connect you to emergency medical assistance.

There is a Medivac air ambulance service (tel: 949 0241) that can fly passengers to hospitals in Miami. For health problems that are not serious, walk-in clinics are available in Grand Cayman. Health care services are excellent, and pharmacies are abundant.

The following numbers may be useful if you need medical care:
Chrissie Tomlinson Memorial Hospital, Grand Cayman, tel: 949 6066.
Cayman Medical and Surgical Center, tel: 949 8150.
Island Chiropractic Center, tel: 945 1988.
Island Medical Associates, tel: 946 3324.
Cayman Dental Services, tel: 945 4447.
Merren Dental Center, tel: 949 2554.
Edmar's Discount Drugs, tel: 949 9800.
Foster's Pharmacy, tel: 945 7759.
Health Care Pharmacy, tel: 949 0442.

CRIME/TROUBLE

With an almost non-existent crime rate, the Cayman Islands is one of the safest places in the Caribbean. It is still advisable not to leave valuables unattended in cars or on the beach. In case of emergency, tel: 911 (toll-free) for both the police and fire departments.

Consulates
Consular assistance is available in Grand Cayman for US citizens (tel: 945 1511) and UK citizens (tel: 949 7900).

COMMUNICATIONS AND MEDIA

Mail
The main post office is on Edward Street in George Town (tel: 949 2474), and a dozen others are scattered throughout the three islands. Most open Mon–Fri 8.30am–5pm. Stamps are also available at most hotels and gift shops.

Telephone/Internet
All the Cayman Islands have excellent telecommunication services, and a large number of fax machines. The area code for all three islands is 345. It is not necessary to dial this code when placing on-island or inter-island calls. Information can be reached by dialing 411.

Local calls are charged by the minute. Public pay phones are located in most commercial areas, and cell phones are available for rent as well.

For calls to the US, US Sprint (888 366 46630), MCI Direct (800 624 1000), and AT&T Direct (800 872 2881) are available. Locally purchased phone cards are convenient, and can be bought at many grocery stores, gas stations, and gift shops.

To place a call to the US, dial 1 + area code + number. To place a call to the UK, dial 011 + 44 + area code + local number. Most major hotels offer high-speed internet hook-up services for guests, or you can use the following internet cafés:
Café del Sol, West Bay Road, Grand Cayman, tel: 946 2233.
McLaughlin's, Village Square, Little Cayman, tel: 948 1000.

Television and Radio
So abundant is cable and satellite television in the Cayman Islands that local people joke about the satellite dish being the national bird. Needless to say, a wide selection of cable television programs from both the United States and the United Kingdom are available in most hotels. There are also two local television channels and eight radio stations that provide news, Caribbean and Country & Western music, current affairs and call-in talk shows, and Christian programs.

practical information

Above: the island crime rate is very low but the police remain vigilant

Newspapers

The Cayman Islands has two daily newspapers, the *Caymanian Compass* (www.caycompass.com) and *Cayman Net News* (www.caymannetnews.com), both have internet editions. The islands also have one weekly newspaper, the *Cayman Observer* (www.caymanobserver.com) and a monthly business broadsheet newspaper, *The Cayman Islands Journal*. Newspapers from the US and the UK can be found at large hotels and bookstores. Several of the larger chain hotels subscribe to the *New York Times* fax service which provides a condensed version of the day's news.

USEFUL INFORMATION

Visitors with disabilities

Most hotels and restaurants are wheelchair-accessible, as are transportation vans from the airport. For special assistance, Elite Limousine Service (tel: 949 5963) is available for transportation, and the Health Care Pharmacy (tel: 949 0442) is a useful, specialized store.

Children

Most major resorts offer baby-sitting services, activities for children, and special programs for teenage visitors. Child-friendly places include several district parks dotted around Grand Cayman, such as Scholar's Park in West Bay; The Dart Family Park on South Church Street in George Town; Captain George Dixon Park at East End, and Jarold Smith Park, North Side.

Also worth a try is the Black Pearl Skate and Surf Park, Grand Harbour Centre, Grand Cayman, tel: 947 4161.

SPORT

Although scuba diving and snorkeling are the sports of choice, golf, fishing, horseback riding, sailing, windsurfing, and kayaking are also popular on the islands. Most of the large hotels have their own swimming pools and tennis courts.

Diving/Snorkeling
Grand Cayman:
Abanks Divers, tel: 945 1444.
Aquanauts Diving, tel: 945 1990.
Bob Soto's Diving, tel: 949 2871.
Dive Cayman, tel: 945 5770.
Divers Down, tel: 945 1611.
Don Foster's Dive, tel: 949 5679.
Ocean Frontiers, tel: 947 7500.
Treasure Island Divers, tel: 949 4456.
Cayman Brac and **Little Cayman**: Most resorts on the sister islands offer their own dive services.

Golf
Britannia Golf Club, Grand Cayman, tel: 949 8020.
Links at Safe Haven, Grand Cayman, tel: 949 5988.
Sunrise Family Golf Centre, Grand Cayman, tel: 947 4653.

Horseback riding
Honeysuckle Trails, Grand Cayman, tel: 947 7976.
Nicki's Beach Rides, Grand Cayman, tel: 945 5839.
Pampered Ponies, Grand Cayman, tel: 945 2262.

Fishing
Cayman Islands Angling Club, Grand Cayman, tel: 945 3131.

Above: you don't have to do your own fishing – the George Town Fish Market can supply all you need

Charter Boat Headquarters, Grand Cayman, tel: 945 4340.
Chip-Chip Fishing Charters, Grand Cayman, tel: 947 1093.
Island Girl Charters, Grand Cayman, tel: 947 3029.
Just Fishin', Grand Cayman, tel: 916 0113.

Sailing/Windsurfing/Kayaking
Barefoot Water-sports, Cayman Brac, tel: 948 1299.
Cayman Kayak Adventures, Grand Cayman, tel: 926 1234.
Cayman Windsurf, Grand Cayman, tel: 947 7492.
Red Baron Charters, Grand Cayman, tel: 945 4744.
Red Sail Water-sports, Grand Cayman, tel: 945 5965.
Sailboards Caribbean, Grand Cayman, tel: 949 1068.
Seasports, Grand Cayman, tel: 949 3965.

Parasailing
Parasailing Professionals, Grand Cayman, tel: 916 2953.

Bowling
Stingray Bowling Center and Arcade, Grand Cayman, tel: 945 4444. (Under refurbishment.)

USEFUL ADDRESSES

Tourist Offices
Cayman Islands Department of Tourism
Regatta Business Park, Leeward Two, West Bay Road, PO Box 67GT, Grand Cayman, Cayman Islands, BWI
Tel: 949 0623
www.caymanislands.ky
United Kingdom
6 Arlington Street, London, SW1A 1RE
Tel: 44 (0) 207 491 7771.
USA
420 Lexington Avenue
New York, NY 10170
Tel: 800 346 3313.
Canada, tel: 416 485 1550.
France, tel: 33 1 53 424136.
Germany/Austria/Benelux, tel: 49 69 60 320 94.

Airlines
Cayman Airways, Grand Cayman, tel: 949 2311;
UK, tel: 44 (0) 207 491 7771;
US/Canada, tel: 800 422 9626;
www.caymanairways.com
Island Air, Grand Cayman, tel: 949 0241;
www.islandaircayman.com
Air Jamaica, tel: 949 2300.
American Airlines, tel: 949 0666.
British Airways, tel: 949 2311.
Delta Air Lines, tel: 945 8431.
US Air, tel: 949 7488.

Booking Agents
The following agents offer travel assistance to US and Canadian tourists:
Cayman Islands Reservation Service, tel: 800 235 5888. International Travel and Resorts, tel: 800 223 9815.

FURTHER READING

Adventuring on Cayman Brac, Skip Harper, Heel and Toe Publishers, 2002.
Brief History of the Caribbean, Jan Rogozinski, Facts on File, 1992.
A Continent of Islands, Mark Kurlansky, Addison-Wesley, 1992.
Birds of the Cayman Islands, Patricia Bradley, World Publications, 1985.
Caribbean, James A Michener, Random House, 1989.
Cayman Islands Dive Guide, Stephen Frink, Abbeville Press, 1999.
Cayman Islands, The Martha K Smith, Cuchipanda Inc, 1995.
Cookin' in Little Cayman, Gladys Howard, Little Cayman National Trust, 1996.
Dive Sites of the Cayman Islands, Lawson Wood, Passport Books, 1998.
Flora of the Cayman Islands, G R Procter, Royal Botanic Gardens, 1984.
Guide to the Reef Fish of the Cayman Islands, Rod MacPherson, Nature World Press, 1995.
Hurricane Ivan Survival Stories, Terri Merren, Mill Press, Jamaica, 2005.
Maritime Heritage of the Cayman Islands, Roger C Smith, Univ. Press of Florida, 2001.
Second Wind, Dick Francis, Random House, 2000.

practical information

ACKNOWLEDGEMENTS

10, 11, 12	AKG London
16	**Cayman Islands National Archive**
2/3, 20, 51B, 52, 53T, 54, 58, 59, 65T	**Wolfgang Tins/Terraqua**

Front cover	**Chris A. Crumley/Alamy**
Back cover	**Phil Wood**

Cartography	**Berndtson & Berndtson**

© APA Publications GmbH & Co. Verlag KG Singapore Branch, Singapore

INDEX